Twentieth-Century Battles
Spencer C. Tucker, editor

THE BATTLE OF HELIGO

THE
BATTLE
OF
HELIGOLAND
BIGHT

Eric W. Osborne

INDIANA UNIVERSITY PRESS

BLOOMINGTON AND INDIANAPOLIS

This book is a publication of

Indiana University Press
601 North Morton Street
Bloomington, IN 47404-3797 USA

http://iupress.indiana.edu

Telephone orders 800-842-6796
Fax orders 812-855-7931
Orders by e-mail iuporder@indiana.edu

The paper used in this publication meets the minimum
requirements of American National Standard for Information
Sciences—Permanence of Paper for Printed Library
Materials, ANSI Z39.48-1984.

Manufactured in the United States of America

Library of Congress Cataloging-in-Publication Data

Osborne, Eric W.
The battle of Heligoland Bight / Eric W. Osborne.
p. cm. — (Twentieth-century battles)
Includes bibliographical references and index.
ISBN 0-253-34742-4 (cloth : alk. paper)
1. Helgoland Bight, Battle of, 1914. I. Title. II. Series.
D582.H4O83 2006
940.4'54—dc22
2005031690

1 2 3 4 5 11 10 09 08 07 06

CONTENTS

INTRODUCTION

THE TOPIC OF THE war at sea in World War I generates continued interest among scholars and general readers alike. While histories abound of World War I and specific naval battles within the conflict, the Battle of Heligoland Bight receives only passing attention in most works, in favor of coverage of larger engagements such as the 1915 Battle of Dogger Bank or the 1916 Battle of Jutland. This state of affairs belies the significance of the battle, one of the most important of the war at sea. The Battle of Heligoland Bight was the first major action between the British Grand Fleet and the German High Seas Fleet. It also influenced the strategy and course of the entire war at sea.

This operation, which unfolded on 28 August 1914, was not designed to produce the decisive fleet encounter sought by naval leaders on both sides during the pre-war years. Instead, the British conceived a raid against German light forces that patrolled around Heligoland Island in the North Sea. This small island guarded the entrance to the German High Seas Fleet's major naval anchorage at Kiel. The plan, which was the brainchild of Commodore Roger Keyes, called for a force comprising the submarines under his command, destroyers under Commodore Reginald Tyrwhitt, and two battle cruisers to provide heavy firepower if needed. The mission was to attack German forces around Heligoland in order to impress on the Germans that whenever they conducted operations in the North Sea they would be subject to attack by units of the Royal Navy. On 28 August 1914, the British force engaged the Germans under the command of Rear Admiral Leberecht Maas. The operation, although it was originally a rather simple plan, was complicated from the start by numerous factors. These included fog, which hampered the performance of the British warships, and Rear Admiral Maas's piecemeal commitment of his forces in an effort to engage the British as quickly as possible. The result was not a battle that involved well-organized squadrons, but a series of individual ship engagements conducted in poor visibility. Compounding the confusion was the fact that the British Admiralty, unbeknownst to Keyes and Tyrwhitt, had dispatched additional reinforcements to the area. The poor weather placed these ships at great risk because of the difficulty of identifying whether a ship was a friend or an enemy.

British forces consequently suffered greater damage than the Germans during the first phase of the battle. The conditions under which the battle was fought increasingly exposed the British to greater danger as they protracted it and thereby increased the chance that the main German battle fleet would sortie to Heligoland to join the battle. In an effort to avoid this potential disaster, the British committed their reinforcements, battle cruisers under Vice Admiral David Beatty. These powerful ships tipped the scales in favor of the British. By the end of the day, the Germans had withdrawn with heavy losses.

The losses suffered in relation to the size of the German navy, however, were fairly minor, which accounts in part for the lack of attention given to the Battle of Heligoland Bight. The lack of coverage is also the result of the confusing nature of the battle. Given the fog, ship movements are harder to track in this battle than in most. Numerous books include the Battle of Heligoland Bight as part of a larger study of World War I at sea, but many do not include in-depth discussion. For example, Paul Halpern's A Naval History of World War I, published in 1994 and regarded by many, including myself, as the best work on the subject, provides only a general overview of the battle and states only that it was very confusing and consequently difficult to describe fully in a general naval study of the war. The battle was not one in which opposing fleets squared off in clearly defined squadrons, as in the 1916 Battle of Jutland. Rather, the two sides engaged in a series of single-ship engagements, largely the result of the poor weather that hampered visibility. The historian must consequently devote a great amount of space in his or her work in order to fully describe and examine the entire battle. This does not lend itself to general works on the war at sea. Some more recent books describe the battle in a greater degree of detail, such as Robert Massie in his work Castles of Steel published in 2003, but this coverage still lacks the degree of detail given to other battles such as Jutland.

Some books are able to offer better coverage through their focus on only a segment of the war. The best of these is James Goldrick's The King's Ships Were at Sea, published in 1984, which covers the war at sea from August 1914 to February 1915. Goldrick's analysis is certainly good, but it too lacks the measure of detail that is necessary for a complete understanding of the battle.

Another reason for this lack of detail in these works is the relative absence of data from the German side of the battle. The lack of this information is one reason why a book dedicated to the Battle of Heligoland Bight is necessary. While discussing the conflict through the British perspective is a good path to take for analysis, given that the operation was British and the events of the battle rested largely on their actions, the German side warrants greater examination in order to fully understand how the contest unfolded.

This approach is particularly important because the Battle of Heligoland Bight was one of the decisive battles of the war due to its strategic ramifications for the war at sea. The Battle of Heligoland Bight was hailed in Britain as a major victory, but in reality the losses incurred by the Germans did little to decrease their overall naval strength, inasmuch as the heavier units of the German High Seas Fleet had remained in their anchorages. The true effect of the conflict was a psychological blow to Germany's navy. The impact of the successful British raid was great, as Heligoland guarded the entrance to the principal German naval base of Kiel. German naval planners had always been aware that the Royal Navy was superior in numbers to their own navy. As a result, they had been unwilling to risk their fleet in a major engagement unless under favorable circumstances. The Battle of Heligoland Bight reinforced the fear of a major fleet engagement. Kaiser Wilhelm II, as a result of the battle, placed severe restrictions on his naval commanders concerning their freedom of action in conducting operations at sea. This greatly hampered the fleet's effectiveness when trying to react quickly to movements of the Royal Navy. The kaiser was unwilling to risk his fleet in any major naval action that might entail significant loss. The Battle of Heligoland Bight consequently obviated the chance for the major fleet engagement that both sides had sought at the beginning of the war. Increasingly, the German High Seas Fleet languished at its anchorages, in effect surrendering command of the North Sea to Great Britain and the Entente.

The strategic results of this were profound, as the kaiser's actions largely precluded a major engagement. Naval leaders on both sides had always planned for a decisive fleet encounter. After Heligoland Bight, with two major exceptions, the war in the North Sea largely involved combat between smaller surface units. This allowed for Britain's continued dominance at sea and through it the maintenance of its naval blockade of Germany. The Battle of Heligoland Bight helped to produce the conditions that ensured the blockade's existence throughout the war. This blockade had dire consequences for Germany during the war overall, which makes the Battle of Heligoland Bight a decisive one despite the lack of significant losses. This work endeavors to provide the greatest possible coverage of the Battle of Heligoland Bight and to highlight its effect on the war at sea as a decisive engagement.

This work would not have been possible without the support of a number of people. In addition to the opportunity to write for the series, I am grateful to Dr. Spencer C. Tucker for his professional advice and encouragement. Thanks are also due to my family and friends. My wife, Iana, has been a great source of support, along with my parents, Dr. and Mrs. Larry Osborne, my brother, Mr. Jack E. Osborne, and my extended family.

THE BATTLE OF HELIGOLAND BIGHT

CHAPTER ONE

THE CONTEXT OF
THE BATTLE OF
HELIGOLAND BIGHT

THE NAVAL ARMS RACE AND THE
RESULTING PRE-WAR STRATEGIES OF
GREAT BRITAIN AND GERMANY

T HE BATTLE OF HELIGOLAND BIGHT took place in a war predicated in part on the naval aspirations of one country, Germany, and the determination of Great Britain to maintain its dominance at sea. The events leading up to World War I, the two most important being the Anglo-German naval arms race and the strategies for war produced by Great Britain and Germany as a consequence of the building contest, are crucial to an understanding of the events that unfolded in the opening days of the war. These ultimately set the stage for the opening of the naval war in the North Sea and the Battle of Heligoland Bight, the first fleet engagement between the principal naval combatants of Britain and Germany.

In the years before 1900, few politicians or naval officials in either Great Britain or Germany would have believed that a pitched naval contest between the two powers would unfold in less than twenty years. Britain had maintained its naval dominance of the seas since 1815, with the end of the Napoleonic Wars, in an atmosphere where it was unchallenged primarily because no one power wished to build a navy large enough to challenge the Royal Navy.[1] The formerly great naval power of France, Britain's chief enemy in the Napoleonic Wars, did not rival Britain again at sea until the second half of the nineteenth century. Even then, although the British by 1850 viewed France as its chief rival, France's navy alone did not pose a strategic threat. France's *Jeune École* was in part the reason for the state of France's navy. This school of naval thought arose in 1869 when Captain Baron Louis-Antoine-Richild Grivel wrote a book entitled *De la Guerre Maritime Avant et Depuis les Nouvelles Inventions* (Naval War before and after the New Inventions). Grivel believed that France did not have the economic power to build a navy on par in numbers with Britain's, so he thought that the best strategy against Britain in a naval war was a war on commerce. This approach gained acceptance in the French navy, and by 1886, with the rise of Admiral Theophile Aube as minister of marine, it dictated France's construction program. Aube believed that a fleet comprising vessels smaller than battleships, the capital vessels of the day, could defeat Britain at sea through a war on commerce. In addition, these same vessels could destroy British battleships thanks to the introduction of the self-propelled torpedo in 1868, which had rendered the battleship obsolete. As a result, the French built far fewer battleships in the second half of the nineteenth century than their British rival. The French navy suffered further from the ideological conflict between proponents of the *Jeune École* and traditionalists, who believed in battleships as the core of the fleet, that unfolded in the mid-1890s and into the early twentieth century. As a result, the French navy between 1896 and 1911 slipped from being the second most powerful navy to fourth place.[2] Many of the vessels were one-ship classes built for trial. This led one observer to label the French navy a "fine set of experiments." Nations other than France presented only a moderate threat to Great Britain. Russia, the third most powerful navy in the world in 1860, possessed an impressive fleet by the turn of the twentieth century, but it could not match that of the British. Nor could that of the United States, which did not begin a program of new naval construction until the first years of the twentieth century and therefore did not represent a material challenge. Before 1900, Germany, while on the path to being a great naval power and becoming a source of concern, was not viewed as a significant threat.

British naval officials up to 1904, consequently, viewed the primary threat to Britain's naval supremacy to be France allied with another naval power. This was a great concern following the 1894 alliance between France and Russia. The British subsequently conducted analyses of combined French and Russian naval strength in keeping with the "Two Power Standard," which held that the British Royal Navy had to be strong enough to combat the combined fleets of any two of the world's major naval powers.[3] Strategic plans for a possible war at sea centered on a conflict with France and Russia where naval power decided the issue. Indeed, the British navy had always been Britain's chief weapon owing to the fact that its army was paltry in comparison to continental European powers. In 1901, the combined armies of France and Russia numbered six million troops, whereas Britain fielded only 160,000 troops for its Expeditionary Force at the beginning of World War I.[4] The naval strategy advocated was the same as in wars past: blockade. The naval blockade had been Britain's key weapon since the eighteenth century. It entailed deploying vessels off the coastline of an enemy power with the object of sealing its ports to overseas commerce. The goal was to create economic hardship on the home front, thus damaging the country's war effort and possibly forcing the enemy to sortie its fleet to try to break the blockade. In the latter circumstance, the Royal Navy would then destroy the enemy. In terms of Russia, planning called specifically for a blockade of Russian ports in the Black Sea in order to destroy commerce and divert some Russian military resources to this theater of operations and thereby away from British ground forces. With respect to France, the British envisioned the blockade of French colonies rather than France itself in order to make them "valuable hostages by the use of which a satisfactory peace might be secured."[5] The British also hoped the economic hardship that the blockade would cause the colonies, as most were dependent on French supplies, would result in the French fleet attacking to try to lift the blockade, thus leading to a decisive battle where the Royal Navy could destroy the French fleet.

These plans were drawn up in 1901 and represented one of the last schemes that took into account France and Russia as the primary threats to British security. Increasingly in the early twentieth century, British officials shifted their attention to Germany, which by that time was beginning to pose a direct threat to Britain's naval supremacy. Such a situation had certainly not been envisioned in the years between 1871, when Germany was unified with Prussia at its core, and 1898, when Germany embarked on a new naval construction program. The original German navy was much like Prussia's had been, in the sense that it was designed primarily as a coastal defense force in keeping with the Prussian emphasis on military land power. Indeed, between 1872 and 1888 the navy was commanded by army officers rather than naval officials.[6]

Throughout this age, German politicians, military, and naval personnel viewed France and Russia rather than Britain as their principal opponents in a war where land power would be the dominant consideration. Chief of the Admiralty Lieutenant General Leo von Caprivi, who took power in 1883 and remained in the post until 1890, was committed to the use of the German navy as a coastal defense force. This course was clear in 1883 with the generation of a document entitled "Memorandum Concerning the Further Development of the Imperial Navy." This document held to the maintenance of a coastal defense force comprising largely torpedo boats, in part due to financial restrictions as the majority of the German military budget was devoted to the army. The emphasis on torpedo boats was also touted as a way to redress the dearth in battleships as the torpedo (as the French *Jeune École* believed) could destroy these vessels.[7] This course, approved by the Reichstag in 1884, also corresponded with Chancellor Otto von Bismarck's belief that Germany should not construct a large oceangoing navy. In his view, such an act ran counter to Germany's interests as a dominant land power in Europe and also threatened to antagonize Great Britain. Bismarck correctly believed that any challenge Germany posed to British naval mastery would be viewed as a threat and could lead to strained relations between the two powers. As a result of these considerations, the German navy in 1890 consisted primarily of one coast-defense battleship (completed in 1890 with another seven under construction), ten aging ironclads, a collection of obsolete corvettes that retained rigging from the age of sail in addition to early steam engines, and eighty-six torpedo boats of varying ages and size.[8] Such a force was an inconsequential one versus Britain's, which was based primarily on battleships.

This situation changed through the direction of Kaiser Wilhelm II, who had assumed the throne in 1888 on the death of his father, Friedrich III, who died only weeks after succeeding Kaiser Wilhelm I. The twenty-nine-year-old Wilhelm II believed from an early point in his reign in the construction of a large oceangoing navy for several reasons. From an early age, the new kaiser had an affinity for the navy through his fondness for his British heritage, as he was the grandson of Britain's Queen Victoria. More importantly, however, Wilhelm II was an ardent believer in *Weltpolitik*, being the foreign policy concept of Germany as a key force in world politics. In order to achieve this goal, by 1898 Wilhelm II was firmly committed to the policy of *Weltmacht*, meaning world power, which called for the German pursuit of empire. This latter goal was in keeping with the kaiser's belief that old empires such as those of Spain and Britain were in decline and that Germany must fill the void in keeping with the drive for world power status. The kaiser's policy goals necessitated a large oceangoing fleet. Wilhelm II was particularly convinced of the necessity of such a navy through the teachings of Alfred Thayer Mahan in his 1890 book, *The Influence of Sea Power upon History*. This book had a particular impact on officials in Germany, Britain, and Japan. Mahan asserted that there was no example in history where a great commercial power was able to maintain its economic position without a large navy. In order to be effective, such a fleet had to include battleships at its core in order to defeat an opposing enemy's fleet that comprised the same kind of vessels. Wilhelm II was devoted from the outset of his reign to the construction of such a fleet that could further his goal of *Weltpolitik* and at the same time make Germany "desired as a friend and feared as an enemy."[9] Perhaps the best summary of the kaiser's goals occurred in a speech in 1900 to German army officers. Wilhelm II said: "As My grandfather [did] for the Army, so I will, for My Navy, carry on unerringly and in a similar manner the work of reorganization so that it may also stand on an equal footing with My armed forces on land so that through it the German Empire may also be in a position abroad to attain that place which it has not yet reached."[10] By this time, measures were already under way to achieve the goal set out in his speech.

The first signal of a shift in the strategic vision of the navy was the 1897 appointment of Admiral Alfred von Tirpitz as state secretary of the Imperial Naval Office (*Reichsmarineamt*). This office was responsible for naval construction as well as the administration of the navy. Tirpitz was one of the two principal proponents of *Weltmacht*, the other being Bernhard von Bülow, who between 1900 and 1909 served as chancellor of Germany. Tirpitz was a career naval officer who had entered the service in 1865, with a commission following four years later. He agreed with Wilhelm II on the need for a fleet centered on battleships and endeavored to create such a fleet in an atmosphere that was at first not committed to such an undertaking. One of Tirpitz's strengths, however, was as a politician. He convinced the public that Germany needed a large navy in the event of war in order to protect the country's trade by keeping shipping lanes in the Baltic and North Sea open and by safeguarding lines of communication between Germany and its overseas empire. The latter was poised on the edge of growth owing to Wilhelm II's drive for imperial possessions through the *Weltmacht* policy. He also touted the need for a fleet large enough that a major naval power would not risk an engagement for fear of losing so many ships that it would be vulnerable to a third power or a coalition of powers. This idea, which was a defensive policy, became known as "risk theory" (*Risikogedanken*) and was aimed primarily at Great Britain, as by this time diplomatic tensions were rising between the two powers. Indeed, Tirpitz voiced clearly his considerations behind the risk theory in a secret memorandum on 15 June 1897: that Germany's most dangerous naval enemy was England and that this situation demanded the construction of battleships in the greatest number possible.[11] The kaiser was quite receptive to these opinions. At the same time, though, Wilhelm II's idea for the projection of power around the world through a great fleet was an unwelcome one in London, which viewed Germany increasingly as an imperial competitor. Tirpitz believed that Britain, despite its still being the principal naval power, would have to recognize the power of the "risk fleet" and thereby ease its stance opposing the kaiser's plans for world power.[12]

The first of Tirpitz's successes in regard to a new fleet occurred on 10 April 1898, when the Reichstag approved the First Navy Law. This measure called for the construction of nineteen battleships, eight armored cruisers, twelve large cruisers, and thirty small cruisers by 1 April 1904.[13] Support for this measure was among the German people, in part thanks to Tirpitz's promoting the navy as a source of national pride. An indication of the navy's growing popularity in the eyes of the public was the membership of Germany's Navy League (*Flottenverein*), a lobbying group heavily supported by industrial interests. In November 1899, this organization counted 240,000 people in its membership, which dwarfed leagues in other naval countries.[14] Tirpitz subsequently was able to capitalize on the navy's popularity and pass a Second Navy Law in 1900 that doubled the size of the fleet to thirty-eight battleships, twenty armored cruisers, and thirty-eight smaller cruisers.[15] The production authorized by this law was to offset British construction, in keeping with Tirpitz's belief that the risk fleet, in order to be effective, must attain a ratio of 2:3 in warships, compared with the British Royal Navy. Upon the passage of these two laws, Germany was put on the path to being a great naval power that could potentially rival Britain for naval supremacy.

This fact was eventually realized in Great Britain. While the majority of British politicians and the people in general did not view Germany's first naval law as a threat, the consensus of opinion shifted markedly with the passage of the second. The British, in an atmosphere of growing tension with Germany over the latter's actions for *Weltpolitik* and *Weltmacht*, viewed the second naval law as a threat to the naval supremacy Great Britain had enjoyed since the end of the Napoleonic Wars. Indeed, the country depended on its naval dominance for the maintenance of the empire and for national survival in terms of both the economy and, crucially, the food supply. With the end of trade protectionism for food through the 1846 abolition of the Corn Laws, Britain had steadily become dependent on cheap foodstuffs from abroad. By 1891, the country imported 80 percent of its food annually.[16] The fundamental need for naval superiority was expressed succinctly by Lord Haldane in a meeting with Kaiser Wilhelm II and Admiral Tirpitz in the midst of the arms race. Haldane remarked that "we [are] an island Power dependent for our food supplies on the power of protecting our commerce."[17] The British viewed Germany as a much more potent threat than they had previously considered France and Russia and consequently embarked on a naval arms race that was in part responsible for the state of affairs that produced World War I. This arms race became a more heated one after 1906 with the British introduction, through the work of First Sea Lord John Fisher (1904–1910), of new, technologically advanced ships. These were the *Dreadnought*-type battleship and the battle cruiser type. These ships, with their main armament comprised of a uniform size of gun and being powered by the latest propulsion machinery, rendered previous ships obsolete. In effect, Britain's superiority was wiped away as battle fleets became based primarily on the new type of battleship.

Tensions steadily escalated in the years between 1906 and 1914 over the naval arms race, despite several attempts to retard the pace of the contest itself and thereby diminish the diplomatic rift between the two nations. These endeavors foundered because both sides saw a large navy as being in their national interest. For Britain, the issue was clear, and many British politicians believed that Germany had no cause to build a battle fleet that would merely worsen relations between the two countries. In the words of Arthur Balfour, a prime minister of Great Britain in the early twentieth century, "Without a superior fleet, Britain would no longer count as a world power. Without any fleet at all, Germany would remain the greatest power in Europe."[18] Such words fell on deaf ears in Germany, where a strong navy was equated with the kaiser's policies of *Weltpolitik* and *Weltmacht*. In the kaiser's mind, with his belief in Mahan's principles of naval power, *Weltmacht* was absolutely necessary.

The belief in the need for such a fleet led to the passage of amendments to navy laws that further strained relations between the two countries. The first of these, in 1906, called for a 35 percent increase in naval spending in light of the introduction of the *Dreadnought* battleship. In 1908, another amendment called for Germany to begin construction on three battleships and one battle cruiser each year, which further threatened British numerical superiority in warships of the most powerful type.[19] In early 1912, relations between the two countries reached their lowest ebb when the British learned that Germany intended to further increase naval construction through another amendment. The British reaction to this news was to send a naval mission to Germany to broach the subject of a reduction in naval armament spending. The British government made its feeling on the current situation plain in terms of necessary steps that Germany must take in order to reduce tensions between the two powers. A memorandum delivered to the kaiser on 29 January 1912 by Sir Ernest Cassel on behalf of the British government laid out three stipulations: acceptance of British naval superiority at sea, no further augmentation of the German naval program, and a reduction of that program to the extent possible. In return, the British were willing not only to offer no objection to German aims of *Weltpolitik* and imperial expansion, but also to promote German ambitions where possible.[20]

The kaiser treated this memorandum as an opening for negotiations on the issue of naval construction, and it ultimately led to the February 1912 Haldane Mission of Britain to Germany. At the core of the discussion was Germany's 1912 naval amendment. This mission resulted in some concessions in terms of the rate of naval construction, but did not produce a agreement that led to a diminution of the naval arms race. Ultimately the 1912 naval amendment, passed in the Reichstag on 21 May 1912, was viewed as a great threat to Britain not only because it allowed construction of an additional three battleships, but also as the bill set aside funds for an increase in the numbers of destroyers and submarines of the fleet. Relations continued to cool between Britain and Germany in the wake of this failure, and naval spending continued at a blinding pace, such that by the outbreak of World War I in August 1914, the two nations were the first and second most powerful naval forces in the world. By that time, Britain operated 22 new dreadnoughts, 9 battle cruisers, 121 cruisers of varying types and age, and 221 destroyers. Germany had at its disposal 15 dreadnoughts, 5 battle cruisers, 40 cruisers of varying types, and 90 destroyers.[21] These vessels, augmented by additional units that were completed following the outbreak of the war, would first enter combat against one another in the Battle of Heligoland Bight.

Despite the vast increase in its navy, Germany did not succeed in its aims through the arms race. Indeed, by 1914 the contest exhibited the bankruptcy of Tirpitz's risk fleet idea in two ways. Firstly, in terms of force strength, Germany was never able to create a fleet that could successfully rival that of Great Britain in numbers, owing in part to the stronger economy of Britain, which could support more naval construction than Germany. Secondly, the risk fleet idea failed in terms of its foreign policy goals concerning Britain. Tirpitz had originally touted it as a way to bring the British to treat with Germany as an equal on the international stage in terms of the German drive for *Weltpolitik*. In a best-case scenario, the Germans had hoped that Britain might consider Germany as an ally. The opposite proved true, although in late 1909 Germany did try to negotiate a nonaggression pact with Britain that London refused to adopt. The increase in naval spending alienated Britain from Germany and forced them to alter their foreign policy from "splendid isolation," where Britain had stayed aloof from continental alliances, to active pursuit of alliances to counter the German threat. The first alliance took place outside of Europe through the 1902 Anglo-Japanese Alliance, which allowed Britain to concentrate its forces in home waters, to answer the growth of the German navy, rather than in Asia. By 1914, Britain was a member of the Triple Entente with France and Russia. Britain was only loosely affiliated with the two rather than actually allied, but the implication was clear: if either France or Russia found themselves embroiled in a war with Germany, there was a high chance that Britain would come to their defense. The German plan had made the British navy its principal opponent in a European war in which the North Sea, and Heligoland Bight within it, became the principal theater of operations.

While the naval arms race unfolded, both British and German naval officials increasingly looked to the possibility of such a conflict and endeavored to design strategies that would garner victory in a war at sea. Both sides' strategies rested in part on the popularly held belief that a decisive fleet encounter would decide the issue. Such a view sprang in part from the writing of Alfred Thayer Mahan. In his *Influence of Sea Power on History*, Mahan championed the construction of battle fleets based on battleships to destroy an enemy force. Prior naval history also led people to believe in the likeliness of such an event. Foremost among the examples was the 1805 Battle of Trafalgar, which inaugurated the age of British naval mastery through the virtual destruction of a combined fleet of French and Spanish warships. In truth, the two sides' strategies, which were in a state of constant flux over the years leading up to World War I, ultimately worked against such an occurrence. Aside from the belief in a decisive conflict, one of the few other similarities in the two sides' strategic thinking was that the island of Heligoland would have a role to play in such a war.

The island of Heligoland is only 150 acres in size and rises 180 feet high out of the rough waters of the North Sea. Despite its size, however, Heligoland was of some importance in terms of naval warfare in the North Sea. Its proximity to Germany accounted for this importance. While the island lies 290 miles from Britain's east coast, it is only 15 miles away from the mouths of the Elbe, Jade, Weser, and Eider Rivers, meaning that it sits at the entrance of all of Germany's major waterways and, subsequently, its major ports. In terms of these installations, Heligoland is located 35 nautical miles northwest of Cuxhaven and 43 nautical miles north of the great German port of Wilhelmshaven. In 1807 during the Napoleonic Wars, the island was seized from Denmark by Great Britain to serve as a naval base, but by the late 1880s, Germany wanted to acquire the island. German officials, including Chancellor Otto von Bismarck, recognized the need for the island, not only to defend Germany's ports, but also to guard the western opening of the Kiel Canal that allowed fast transit of German naval units between the North Sea and the great German naval base of Kiel on the Baltic Sea. Construction had begun in 1887 and was ultimately completed eight years later.[22] In 1890, negotiations in the midst of the canal's construction resulted in Britain's ceding the island to Germany. With Heligoland in their possession, the Germans were free to build defenses to safeguard the waters around the island, known as the Heligoland Bight, and thereby safeguard the navy's ports.

The cession of Heligoland was not a foregone conclusion in 1890, because the British realized the strategic importance of the island in the event of a possible war against Germany. Indeed, negotiations had ensued years beforehand, in both 1884 and 1885. At that time, German ambassador to Britain Count Münster had tried to ease British opposition through his ardent belief that "it was as good as impossible that Germany and England should ever be at war . . . the cessation of Heligoland would strengthen the good feeling of Germany towards [Britain] to an extraordinary degree."[23] The cession was possible primarily as it formed part of the African Convention, signed on 1 July 1890, that dealt with matters of empire. Britain gained elsewhere through conceding Heligoland. In exchange for it, Britain secured Germany's withdrawal from some territories in east Africa that included Zanzibar.[24]

This gain certainly proved paltry in the midst of the Anglo-German naval race when British naval officials approached the issue of Heligoland as part of their wider war plans against Germany at sea. Although no concrete offensive strategy versus Germany was placed in writing before 1908, the British had begun as early as 1903 to contemplate a war with the Germans. Central to the British was their belief in a decisive action at sea. This goal was encapsulated in the 1 July 1908 War Orders to the Commander in Chief of Britain's Channel Fleet, which at the time was the country's naval force assigned to home waters: "The principal object is to bring the main German Fleet to decisive action, and all other operations are subsidiary to this end."[25] The earliest writings on the method to achieve this focused primarily on the Royal Navy's past practice of closely blockading an enemy's ports in order to damage the nation's economy, and thereby its capacity to fight. British calculations on the value of German commerce reveal the importance attached to such an endeavor. A February 1903 report composed for the Committee of Imperial Defense (CID), an organization charged with advising the government on strategic policy, entitled "The Military Resources of Germany, and Probable Method of their Employment in a War between Germany and England" pointed out that Germany's merchant marine was the second largest in the world.[26] The British believed that cutting off this commerce, in combination with the seizure of contraband on neutral vessels passing to Germany, could damage the German war effort. Naval policy rested on the value of blockade and resulted in a CID memorandum days after the report on the military resources of Germany. This document, entitled "Memorandum on the Military Policy to Be Adopted in a War with Germany," concluded that any military action through a ground assault on Germany proper would be impossible given Germany's vast ground forces in comparison to the British army. The only course open to Britain against Germany was the destruction of the enemy's seaborne trade. Notably, as part of this endeavor, the memorandum recommended the seizure of Heligoland Island as a base of operations for close blockade. Clearly, Heligoland Island occupied a position of importance in British naval planning from the earliest stage.[27] As in the past, naval officials hoped that a close blockade would force the enemy fleet to sortie in order to try to lift the blockade and thereby stave off economic and military ruin. The British assumed that their fleet's numerical superiority would result in a victory against Germany in the decisive battle that most of the British believed would ensue. This plan not only was in keeping with past British practice, but also was the one that the Germans ardently believed that the British would execute in time of war.

Increasingly, however, naval officials in Britain began to realize that the time-honored strategy of the Royal Navy was difficult to execute, bordering on impossible in the early twentieth century. Advances in naval technology were the collective cause of the problem, and numerous naval officials grasped the quandary as early as the late nineteenth century. By the early twentieth century, first sea lord of the Admiralty (1904–1910) Admiral John Fisher also ranked among those that appreciated the problem. His interest in technology, which had yielded the *Dreadnought*-type battleship, led him to see that in the case of a continental European enemy, the old strategy of close blockade was a bankrupt policy. In his mind, the invention of such weapons as the self-propelled torpedo and advances in mine warfare in the second half of the nineteenth century meant that the Royal Navy had to avoid the permanent proximity to the German coast that close blockade required. In such a case, the Germans would be able to inflict a great deal of damage at cheap cost through the use of the new weaponry. Fisher first responded to the problem in 1908 through operational orders that called for a close blockade only during the day. At night, the major units of the fleet would withdraw 170 miles from the nearest German naval base harboring destroyers, while smaller craft remained 30 miles off the coast to monitor German movements.[28] Even this arrangement was eventually viewed as impractical by many naval officials, including Fisher. By 1910, the year of his departure as first sea lord, Fisher advocated the implementation of a distant blockade of Germany in which the Royal Navy would stay out of the southern waters of the North Sea altogether.[29] Even so, upon the end of Fisher's tenure, the war plans had not fully addressed the problem with Britain's principal weapon at sea. This scheme, which gave up the use of close blockade while not clearly establishing a new strategy in its place, is a clear indication of the differences of opinion prevailing in the Admiralty itself.

The relative crisis in British strategic thought continued in the age after Fisher through the appointment of Admiral Sir Arthur Wilson as first sea lord (1910–1911). He is a prime example of the British struggle to create a viable naval strategy for a war with Germany. Wilson, Fisher's handpicked successor, originally supported the idea of a distant blockade, but quickly reverted to the concept of a close blockade at the beginning of his tenure. His advocacy of this plan and the ideological split over strategy culminated in a meeting of the CID on 23 August 1911 to discuss an overall military strategy for war against Germany. Wilson believed that British offensive operations in general should rest on the shoulders of the navy and called for a close blockade of the entire North Sea coast to that end. He also renewed the old call for the capture of Heligoland, for use not only as a forward base of operations for the blockade, but also as a staging point for possible amphibious assaults to capture German ports such as Wilhelmshaven. That viewpoint represented one school of thought in the wider strategic debate unfolding at the time over the general direction of Britain's war effort. Wilson, and Fisher before him, believed in the classic model of the Royal Navy transporting the army, in this case to some area of the German coast, for use in amphibious attacks, while others believed in the continental strategy of the army that called for the Royal Navy to support the transport of the entire British Expeditionary Force to France in the opening days of the war for joint operations. Firmly in the amphibious school of thought, Wilson asserted that the capture of German ports would both cripple the naval power of the Germans and serve as a diversion for the French in the ground war on the European front.[30]

Opposition to this plan, primarily the emphasis on close blockade, was voiced by several of the other members of the committee, including Home Secretary Winston Churchill, Lord Haldane, and Sir John French of the British Army General Staff. The matter had not been resolved by the end of Wilson's tenure in November 1911; in the same month as his dismissal from office the first sea lord issued war orders to then commander in chief of the Home

Fleet Admiral Sir George Callaghan to institute a close blockade of Germany in the event of war. Callaghan's response was to strongly object to the orders and ask for a review by the Admiralty of the decision for a close blockade.[31] By the time the admiral voiced his concern, there was a change in the administration of the Admiralty, and they were willing to listen.

In October 1911, Winston Churchill assumed the office of First Lord of the Admiralty, the highest post in the naval organization. He appointed Admiral Francis Bridgeman as first sea lord in November 1911, and the two formulated a strategy that brought the Royal Navy back to the policy of a distant blockade that avoided the use of British warships in the southern North Sea near Germany's coasts. In the first drafts of the 1912 war plans, Churchill envisioned an observational line of cruisers that ran from the coast of Norway to the British eastern coast around Newcastle-upon-Tyne. While Churchill had lingering doubts about the effectiveness of such a system, he did believe that it was the only solution in the face of the problems inherent in a close blockade. His doubts about the value of the distant blockade did not matter greatly given that he attached the greatest significance to luring out and destroying the German battle fleet through the pressure of the blockade rather than entirely destroying Germany's trade.[32] Churchill's plan was modified in the beginning of July 1914 so that the line of cruisers forming the blockade was moved farther north in order to patrol the entrance to the North Sea between the Orkney Islands and the coast of Norway. The objective of causing some degree of economic hardship to entice the German fleet to sortie and fight remained the primary consideration. The Grand Fleet, the main portion of the Royal Navy by this time, was tasked with conducting sweeps into the northern North Sea in expectation of meeting the German force. The Royal Navy entered action in World War I with this strategy at the center of their operations.

While this plan obviated the need to capture the island of Heligoland for naval purposes, the idea of doing so continued to surface within the Admiralty in the final years leading up to World War I. This happened largely because of Churchill, who despite his opposition to Wilson's call of close blockade in 1911 attached value to the endeavor as a means of garnering a forward base of operations. In 1913, Churchill had instructed Admiral Lewis Bayly to work with both Admiral John Fisher and Admiral Arthur Wilson to this end. He even went so far as to have plaster models constructed of the island for the purpose of planning an amphibious assault. The plan, however, was shelved as a result of the opening of the war and after a report on 11 August 1914 showed such a plan would be too costly in men and material.[33] In addition, by this time the other great strategic debate for the British, that of whether to pursue amphibious warfare or a continental strategy, had been resolved in favor of the latter.

As Britain wrestled with the question of strategy that included the consideration of Heligoland, so too did Germany. Indeed, the process was just as torturous, but produced far less satisfactory results. The Germans first drew up plans for a naval war against Britain in 1896 in reaction to the fallout over an imperial conflict. As Africa was being carved up among several European powers, including Germany as part of the kaiser's *Weltpolitik*, an event unfolded in Britain's Cape Colony in South Africa that led to strained relations between the two powers. The incident that precipitated the problem was the December 1895 Jameson Raid. Without London's knowledge, six hundred men under the command of Dr. Leander Starr Jameson, with the support of British entrepreneur Cecil Rhodes, invaded the Transvaal Republic of the Dutch Boers. The object was to make a raid into the republic in the name of defending British migrant workers there who were supposedly being harassed, with the actual goal to annex the territory, which held massive diamond deposits, into the British Empire. The Boers, who were supported by Wilhelm II, defeated the raiders. On 3 January 1896, the kaiser telegraphed his congratulations to Transvaal Republic president Paul Kruger, which was immediately interpreted by the British as direct interference by Germany in Britain's imperial affairs. Amidst the widespread public outcry that the event generated, the British government on 7 January 1896 created a "flying squadron" comprising two battleships, four cruisers, and four destroyers that could be deployed anywhere in the empire that an emergency might arise.[34] Although this squadron was disbanded in October 1896, its existence revealed the fact that at this time the German navy could not counter such actions effectively because of the relatively small size of the fleet. This realization in part would drive the kaiser to take up the idea of *Weltmacht* through Tirpitz's plan for a risk fleet.

The appointment of Tirpitz as state secretary of the Imperial Naval Office, however, did not come to pass until 16 June 1897, as the kaiser at the time was not of the mind to fully embrace Tirpitz's proposals. Instead, Wilhelm II sided with those who not only advocated caution in the face of Great Britain, but also pointed out that the Reichstag at the time was not supportive of increased naval spending. In addition, then state secretary Admiral Friedrich von Hollman was able in March 1896 to secure limited funds for the construction of four new warships, which partly assuaged the kaiser's desire for more naval units.[35]

Despite the lack of a significant increase in German naval production in answer to Britain, the affair of the Jameson Raid and subsequent Kruger Telegram signaled the beginning of a shift in German naval strategic planning. Neither government or naval officials viewed Britain as the chief threat to Germany in Europe, believing that the key concern of the country in terms of military planning should be the continental powers of France and Russia, in keeping with policy that had been in place through former Chancellor Bismarck since the unification of Germany. Even so, rising tensions with Britain forced some consideration of war with that country. In the wake of the imperial clash, commanding admiral of the navy Eduard von Knorr of the Admiralty High Command commissioned Rear Admiral Otto von Diederichs, his chief of staff, to draft plans for employment of the navy in a possible war with Britain. These plans revolved around the central question of whether to pursue an offensive or defensive strategy against Britain and, by extension, where to position the fleet to achieve the ultimate goal of victory. In the beginning, the superior size of the British Royal Navy over that of Germany dictated the nature of the plans, the first being offensive in nature. On March 5 1896, Commander August von Heeringen under Diederichs's direction initiated the study of the matter with his memorandum "Concepts for an operations plan of our warships in a war between Germany alone and Britain alone."[36] This report was predicated on the fact that Germany was greatly outnumbered by Britain in numbers of warships. Heeringen assumed, as did most German naval officials, that Britain would employ its strategy of close blockade in the opening days of the war. As the German navy could not hope to counter such a strong force, Heeringen believed that the only way to keep Britain from dominating the North Sea, and Germany from having its trade routes consequently severed, was to rapidly mobilize the German navy and strike against all British shipping in the Thames River before the Royal Navy had concentrated for action. This seemed possible given that a great deal of the Royal Navy at the time was deployed to different areas of Britain's vast empire. Heeringen believed that this attack might lead those few units of the Royal Navy that had mobilized to sortie in a piecemeal fashion rather than in a concentrated force to try to protect the shipping of the Thames. This would give the German navy temporary control of the North Sea in order to build up coastal forces and mine the southern North Sea to better resist the inevitable British counterattack that would ensue. In a memorandum on 23 April 1896, Diederichs expanded on Heeringen's proposal. He proposed additional measures such as mining British ports and using commerce raiders to attack British coastal trade, to be used in combination with the strike on the Thames. He went further to say that this strategy, if it was successful, might disrupt the British economy to such a point that Britain could be forced to sue for peace.[37] If that did not result, then he believed that coastal defense had to be shored up as much as possible to resist the inevitable British close blockade. In his mind, the German navy had to "offer battle only in case of favorable conditions and at a time of our choosing" in an effort to break the blockade.[38]

The plan advocated by Diederichs and Heeringen, however, suffered from faults. One of these was recognized by another staff officer, who wrote in response to Heeringen's proposal that "England will never declare war before she has collected a fleet of overwhelming superiority in the Channel or off the Thames. Under such conditions this sort of offensive thrust would be worthless."[39] Diederichs himself recognized this fact when he prefaced his strategic remarks with the assertion that war with Britain must be avoided at all costs. In his mind, due to Britain's numerical superiority, the German navy could realistically hope only for a prolonged struggle that would ultimately end in German defeat.

Even so, Admiral von Knorr believed that this early plan was the better option as opposed to assuming a defensive position in the North Sea and waiting for the British to attack and institute a close blockade to destroy German commerce. The 1896 naval maneuvers consequently became the first in which the German fleet envisioned not only war with France and Russia, but also a possible one with Britain. This operation, however, represented the infancy of any plan against Britain as politicians, such as Friedrich von Holstein of the Foreign Office, favored pursuing a guarded, friendly policy to Britain in the hope of someday forming an alliance with the island nation. The kaiser envisioned the same and considered a war with Britain unthinkable. Only in May 1897 did Admiral Knorr, in an audience with the kaiser, broach the subject again in an audience in part to discuss strategic planning. In his thinking, Heeringen and Diederichs's plan offered the possibility of an invasion of England if, in the initial attack on the Thames, German naval forces were able to destroy most of the British fleet while it was still mobilizing.[40] This idea, however, proved stillborn for three reasons. Firstly, it required joint planning with the army, as Knorr envisioned using Dutch or Belgian territory as embarkation points for the invasion force. The army believed that, barring an alliance with either the Netherlands or Belgium, it would take too long to conquer these areas for use in such an operation. The general staff believed that an invasion force would have to quickly force Britain to surrender, or else the force would be cut off from supply and defeated when more British warships arrived from points in the empire. The general staff pointed out that these British vessels in combination would gradually overwhelm the smaller German navy and reestablish the naval supremacy of Britain in the North Sea. The second problem was a political one. In the eyes of German politicians, the overrunning of the Netherlands or Belgium would prove costly for various reasons.[41] Finally, British organizational reforms in their fleet rendered the plan unworkable. In 1897, the British augmented the size of their fleet in the region of the North Sea through redistributing some warships between the various stations of the empire. This move meant that the German navy would be facing a more concentrated Royal Navy, and more units would have to be engaged for decisive victory. Knorr was forced to accept that under this new circumstance, there was little hope that the plan would succeed.[42] As a result, the first naval plan against Britain was shelved.

Naval planning for a war against Britain resumed and assumed a new direction, following the thinking of secretary of state for foreign affairs Bernhard von Bülow, with his ideas of *Weltmacht*, and particularly with the appointment of Admiral Alfred Tirpitz, who also believed in the principle, as state secretary of the Imperial Naval Office in July 1897. Tirpitz, through his new office, was responsible only for naval administration and construction rather than planning.

Nevertheless, as his idea of a risk fleet found favor with the kaiser as a means to achieving *Weltpolitik*, Tirpitz wielded enormous power. He alone also was primarily responsible, through his naval laws, for the construction of the new fleet. Consequently, Tirpitz had a role to play in how the new fleet would be used.[43]

Tirpitz's risk fleet was first and foremost designed as a deterrent, primarily against Britain, in that the threat of such a fleet would permit the kaiser to safely pursue his policy of *Weltpolitik*. Nevertheless, Tirpitz recognized the need for naval war plans against Britain, as he foresaw a period of danger during the construction of the fleet—that period when the navy did not have enough vessels to deter Britain, during which the British might choose to attack and destroy the new naval force. Tirpitz's ideas for a war against Britain ran completely counter to the concept of an offensive operation such as Knorr's, which envisioned an invasion of the British Isles. The admiral echoed the sentiments of others that an invasion of Britain would not succeed. In fact, Tirpitz characterized the idea as "insane." The very concept of his fleet played to a defensive rather than an offensive strategy; this is evident through Tirpitz's description of the risk fleet. Tirpitz advocated the construction of a battle fleet whose size and power would discourage naval powers from seeking battle against it: "Germany must have such a strong battle fleet that a war even with the greatest sea power would carry with it such risks that her own predominance would be endangered."[44] This policy, however, was aimed directly at Britain as the greatest naval power and necessitated a strategy in the event of war. Indeed, Tirpitz's earlier writings in 1894, before he assumed office, had dealt with the idea of a great battle fleet that could in theory break any blockade of its shores if necessary.[45] Tirpitz asserted that the decisive actions in a naval war with Britain would take place in the region of Heligoland Bight when the British arrived to institute their close blockade. Considerations in the Tirpitz era reflected the admiral's thinking as Germany embarked on the construction of its new battle fleet.

In 1899, the new strategy as presented to the kaiser abandoned an invasion of Britain. This plan called for dealing with the assumed close blockade of Britain and British naval supremacy in general by withdrawing the German fleet to Kiel in the Baltic and by acquiring, through force or diplomacy, access to Denmark in order to protect the entrance into the Baltic. German officials thought that the British might not launch operations into the region of Heligoland Bight for fear of an attack by German naval forces from the Baltic.[46] This plan, like its predecessor, was stymied in part by the army, which was opposed to any operation in Denmark. The general staff was solely occupied with potential operations against France and Russia and saw this plan as a diminution of their force strength to that end.[47] After much wrangling between the services, by 1904 the army war staff completely rejected the scheme.

By 1904 the army general staff stood firmly against the tenets of the 1899 proposal as the plan proved unworkable given developments stemming from the building naval arms race between Britain and Germany. Increasingly, German naval officials were forced to face the possibility of far greater numbers of enemy warships arrayed against them than had been the case in prior planning. In response to the arms race generated by Tirpitz's plan, Britain in 1904 partially reorganized its fleet in order to concentrate more of it in the North Sea against Germany. The measure was made possible in part through a 1902 alliance between Britain and Japan, in which Britain relied on their partner to protect the empire's commerce in Asia. This allowed for the removal of British vessels from far-flung outposts. The new distribution meant that Britain would have at its disposal three-quarters of its battleships for a war with Germany.[48] The numbers also worsened for Germany in the same year through the conclusion of the Entente Cordiale between Britain and France. While not a firm alliance, the entente signaled a warming of relations between the two powers, which Germany viewed as being directed against it. Indeed, the British view of Germany as a rising threat had made the Entente possible. In the event of war, Germany might face both the British and French fleets. The situation grew still worse in 1907 when the same type of agreement was concluded between Britain and Russia. These steps combined to wholly undermine the risk fleet idea as the British would have at their disposal forces to execute operations against Germany that could easily overwhelm the German fleet.

As a result of the collapse of the 1899 plan, German naval officials were forced to reconsider the strategy with Britain amidst conditions that made the position of the fleet in war increasingly unfavorable. In light of this situation, in early 1905 proposals continued to concentrate on Britain as the principal enemy, but centered on a new defensive strategy in which the island of Heligoland and the Heligoland Bight assumed importance. In keeping with the continued belief that Britain would institute a close blockade of Germany's shores, the Germans advocated placing the battle fleet in the region of Heligoland Bight and in the principal naval bases in the North Sea. This plan, therefore, was the first that focused a much greater attention on building up the defenses and installations of Heligoland as well as other naval installations in the North Sea. Upon the outbreak of war, the fleet would adhere to a defensive strategy and engage the British near the German coast in conditions most favorable for victory. The Germans hoped that through a series of these engagements, conducted largely with submarines and torpedo boats, they could maintain the majority of their fleet intact while whittling down the numerical superiority of the British. Once the German and British battle fleets were virtually equal in numbers, the German fleet would engage the British in a decisive battle for naval superiority in the North Sea.[49] The German naval command reasoned that even if this battle did not result in German victory, British losses might be so great as to render an effective close blockade difficult to impossible.

This plan found favor in part because it seemed the only option still available that offered any chance of success against the British navy. It also had the advantage of fitting in well with political considerations concerning the use of the fleet in a war. Many of Germany's statesmen, including the kaiser, held that the fleet must be kept intact as a diplomatic tool in negotiations to end a conflict. The maintenance of such a fleet, they asserted, would be a powerful source of strength that could improve Germany's position in such talks.[50] Indeed, the idea of seeking battle only under conditions that were most favorable was predicated in part on this political desire.

Unfortunately for the Germans, this planning did not signal an end to the question of how best to combat the British navy. Increasingly, the problem was a growing doubt concerning the principal assumption underlying the strategy: the British execution of a close blockade strategy. As a result of this concern, in 1908 a new plan was produced that advocated an offensive rather than defensive strategy. By this time, the British were indeed in the process of wrestling with the viability of close blockade in modern war. British naval maneuvers reflected the changing thought in the Admiralty, and consequently led the Germans to consider that a close blockade might not occur at all. As a result, chief of the Admiralstab Vice Admiral Friedrich von Baudissin sensed that the British might employ a distant blockade and advocated the use of the German navy to attack the distant light forces with the entire fleet if necessary. The primary object remained reducing the strength of the British navy as a prelude to a decisive battle.

Kaiser Wilhelm II was swayed by this plan and endorsed it, leading to its continued survival under the guidance of Admiral Max von Fischel, who was Baudissin's successor. Fischel summed up the position of Germany and the need for an offensive strategy in 1910 when he wrote, "In the final analysis we are fighting for access to the ocean, whose entrances . . . are in England's hands. However the war may be fought, we are therefore basically that attacker, who is disputing the enemy's possession."[51] This statement, however, was made at a time when Fischel's strategy had been undermined by other forces in the German naval administration. The appointment in 1909 of Vice Admiral von Holtzendorff as commander in chief of the German High Seas Fleet accounted for this fact. Holtzendorff asserted that he did not have enough vessels for such offensive operations to succeed. Consequently, a compromise was reached where the High Seas Fleet would assume a waiting offensive rather than an all-out attack at the beginning of the war. In effect, this compromise signaled a return to a defensive strategy.

The arguments between Holtzendorff and the Admiralstab staff dominated strategic considerations for two years following the compromise, in a situation where German naval strategy against Britain clearly needed revision. By 1912, the operational orders of the High Seas Fleet, approved by the kaiser, were

largely those of 1905 in terms of being a defensive strategy based on the fundamental idea of Britain's establishing a close blockade in the North Sea:

> His Majesty the Emperor has ordered the following for the conduct of war
> in the North Sea:
>
> 1. The aim of the operations should be to damage the British fleet through
> offensive advances against the patrol or blockade forces of the German
> Bight . . . and when possible submarine offensives carried as far as the
> English coast.
>
> 2. After an equalization of forces has been accomplished by this conduct
> of the war, it is desired that our fleet seek to engage in battle under favorable
> circumstances after preparation and gathering together of all forces. If prior
> to this a favorable opportunity to engage offers itself, it should be taken ad-
> vantage of.[52]

The 1913 fleet exercises rested on the execution of these war orders versus a
close blockade of Britain. The Germans assumed that the British would choose
Heligoland Bight as the basis for their operations and that they would sortie immediately in search of a decisive battle, in keeping with the past tradition of the
British Royal Navy.

The exercises revealed the possibility that the war orders rested on a mistaken assumption in terms of close blockade. Vice Admiral Ingenohl, who became commander in chief of the High Seas Fleet in 1913, as well as other naval
officers in the fleet and officials of the Admiralty Staff, recognized that the fleet
exercises belied the use of close blockade. The maintenance of a close blockade
by the British was found to be extremely costly for the British in the age of
newer, more capable weaponry. If this proved true and Britain chose a different
strategy, it would undermine the first stipulation of the war orders and ultimately the German war effort at sea. By 1914, officers in the High Seas Fleet
were "firmly convinced that the British fleet would not risk such a 'close' blockade, but would, instead, substitute a 'distant' blockade. The Admiralty Staff
moreover concluded that in such a distant blockade the British Fleet would uti-
lize Scapa Flow as its main base."[53] The implementation of such a distant
blockade at the mouth of the North Sea and the placement of the British navy
at Scapa Flow, situated in the Orkney Islands in the extreme north of the British Isles and North Sea, would render the 1912 war orders of little use. The war
orders assumed a war unfolding in the southern half of the North Sea rather
than the distant north. No one seemed to have the answer to this problem. A
poignant example of the problem came in the midst of the debate over Britain's
probable strategy when Tirpitz asked von Ingenohl, "What will you do if they
do not come?" Neither von Ingenohl or Tirpitz had a satisfactory answer.[54]

The question of whether or not the British would employ a close or distant
blockade was never settled satisfactorily by the German naval command in the

years leading to the outbreak of World War I. As a result, the July 1914 directives issued on the eve of the conflict represented a hybrid of the 1912 plan that attempted to deal with both types of blockade. The basic directives of the 1912 orders remained intact, but in addition chief of the Admiralty Staff Admiral Hugo von Pohl called for an attack on a distant blockade by submarines and minelayers. While these forces engaged the distant blockade, Pohl directed that the main elements of the High Seas Fleet would attack any British warships in Heligoland Bight that were attempting to institute a close blockade or were simply guarding the bight. The ultimate object remained whittling down the numerical superiority of the British with the object of achieving near parity and victory through a subsequent decisive battle. Even by 1914, many naval officers felt that the mixed strategy present in the directives was not a cause of alarm. In the words of one officer: "There was an opinion among us, from the Commander-in-Chief down to the latest recruit, about the attitude of the English Fleet. We were convinced that it would seek out and attack the Fleet the minute it showed itself and wherever it was."[55] That belief rested on use of a close blockade rather than one that would remove the British fleet from Germany's shores. The highest-ranking naval officials clung to the belief that the strategy was not a cause for concern for a political reason as well. They believed that Germany's political leaders would never allow the country to become embroiled in a war with Britain.

In essence, Germany entered World War I with no clearly defined naval strategy. The last set of war directives assumed that the British would at least deploy some forces to guard Heligoland Bight if not to institute a close blockade altogether. They overlooked, however, the possibility that in the event of a distant blockade the British might not send any forces at all.[56] Such a situation would consign the High Seas Fleet to inaction while Britain retained mastery of the sea. This situation proved to be exactly how the war at sea unfolded, as German forces were stationed in their North Sea ports waiting for a massed assault that did not come. Without the benefit of hindsight, however, German light forces were attached to the defense and reconnaissance of Heligoland Bight to warn of the coming of such an attack and provide time for the heavy units of the High Seas Fleet to react to it.

Upon the outbreak of war between Britain and Germany on 4 August 1914, the execution of this confused, vague strategy as well as Great Britain's rested with the naval administrations of the two countries. While Britain and Germany benefited from several politicians and naval officials of worth, they suffered from a number of bureaucratic drawbacks that had a direct effect on the events that unfolded up to and during the Battle of Heligoland Bight.

The naval administration of Great Britain labored under a convoluted system of leadership in which strategic policy was the responsibility of two organizations under the government of Prime Minister Herbert Asquith: the Admiralty, the original naval administration of the British navy, and the Naval War Staff (also known as the Admiralty War Staff), which was a body within it. The Admiralty traced its origin back to 1546, when King Henry VIII created the Navy Board.[57] By 1914, it was headed by a first lord of the Admiralty, who was a civilian and a cabinet minister in the government. At the outbreak of World War I Winston Churchill held the position. Born in 1874, Churchill had already been involved in British national politics for fourteen years and had overseen the move toward a distant blockade that had developed by the beginning of the war. Churchill as first lord was responsible for overseeing the Board of Admiralty, which consisted of four sea lords. The first sea lord was the most influential and gave advice on naval policy as well as information on the composition and disposition of the fleet. This individual was Prince Louis Battenberg, who had held the office since 1912 and was generally regarded as a fine naval officer. The second sea lord dealt with the personnel and the mobilization of the fleet, while the third sea lord dealt with the procurement of all naval ordnance and equipment. The fourth sea lord dealt with the transport of supplies.

By the outbreak of World War I, the original Board of Admiralty, being the first lord and the sea lords, was not the dominant body overseeing naval operations. This duty fell to the Naval War Staff, which was a creation of First Lord Churchill. The problematic 23 August 1911 meeting of the Committee of Imperial Defense had prompted its creation. This meeting had produced great disagreement over not only the issue of close blockade, which then First Sea Lord Wilson had tried to reinstate over distant blockade, but also the issue of the overall military approach to a war versus Germany. In terms of the latter, an argument had erupted specifically over whether to employ an amphibious policy against Germany, meaning amphibious assaults against the German coastline, or a continental strategy that called for the Royal Navy to support the transport of the British Expeditionary Force to France to serve with French units. The decision to adopt a continental strategy had led the Asquith government to order the Admiralty to assist the War Office, in charge of army operations, in drawing up plans for a joint operation. When members of the Admiralty, still in favor of the amphibious strategy, dragged their feet, Asquith called for administrative reform in the Admiralty, which led Churchill to create the Naval War Staff.

The leadership of this administrative body, created in 1912, comprised the first lord, first sea lord, chief of the War Staff Admiral Doveton Sturdee, and a secretary. Although at first designed to be merely an advisory panel within the Admiralty itself, the staff through the leadership of Churchill became the command structure for the navy during the war. The organization was separated into three divisions: operations, intelligence, and mobilization. Its mission sprang from Churchill's argument that the necessities of modern warfare made essential a staff body tasked with overseeing all operations in time of war. In his

mind, the staff was to be "a brain far more comprehensive than any one man.
. . . It is to be an instrument capable of formulating any decision which has to
be taken, or may be taken, by the Executive in terms of precise and exhaustive
detail."[58] Such centralization of the operational aspect of the navy met with
much resistance; in past British history it had been left to admirals to conduct
specific operations, with only general orders defining their actions. Former first
sea lord Wilson, echoing the sentiments of many, saw the staff system as being
simply incompatible with the navy in terms of its requirements: "a Naval War
Staff is an attempt to adapt to the Navy a system which was primarily designed
for the army."[59] With this statement, Wilson touched on the assertion that such
a system for the navy had the potential to prove vastly inefficient and compromise naval operations in the event of war.

This idea proved to be accurate and explains in large part many of the errors
committed by the naval command in World War I, including several in the Battle
of Heligoland Bight that nearly resulted in disaster for the Royal Navy. As the
staff came into being only two years before the start of the war, many key members did not know fully their duties. Rear Admiral H. G. Thursfield, who served
in the operations division, laid this problem bare in his comments on the conduct of the Naval War Staff in the first months of the war:

> Neither the Chief of the War Staff nor the Director of Operations Division
> [Admiral Sir Arthur Leveson] seemed to have any particular idea what the
> War Staff was supposed to be doing, or how they should make use of it; they
> had been brought up in the tradition that the conduct of the fleet was a mat-
> ter for the admiral alone, and that he needed no assistance in assimilating
> the whole situation and its ramifications, and in reaching a decision, probably
> instantaneously, upon what should be done and what orders should be is-
> sued in order to get it done.[60]

Adding to the leaders' confused purpose of the staff was the lack of experience
of many of the people within it. Unlike the admirals in the upper echelons,
those beneath had little experience in detailed study of naval warfare. Arguably
this includes First Lord Churchill, as he was a civilian, had been educated at
Sandhurst Military Academy, and had served consequently in the army rather
than the navy. By 1911, despite the ardor for naval affairs that he held by this
time, Churchill was still not as seasoned as regular naval officers in the art of
naval warfare. Also, the staff lent itself to such a degree of centralization that it
rarely included the other lords of the Admiralty, and it even tried to direct operations at sea by wireless communication. Indeed, commander in chief of the British navy Admiral John Jellicoe encountered this problem, to his vexation, on
more than one occasion. Finally, the Naval War Staff believed in such a degree
of secrecy that oftentimes the commanders of operations themselves were not
fully aware of the details of the mission.[61] In sum, this bureaucracy made it quite

difficult to coordinate actions between the Admiralty and forces at sea. The Battle of Heligoland Bight starkly demonstrated this problem.

While Jellicoe and others within the British navy chaffed under the Naval War Staff, their problems did not compare to those of the German High Seas Fleet through their naval administration. In 1914, commander in chief of the High Seas Fleet Admiral Friedrich von Ingenohl labored under a greatly more complicated system that limited his degree of action far more than Jellicoe with the Naval War Staff. This situation was the product of changes made to the governing apparatus of the navy over the course of Kaiser Wilhelm II's reign. Throughout the era of Bismarck and in the first years of Wilhelm's rule, the navy was merely a branch of the army in terms of its control. A flurry of steps at reorganization came in 1889 when Wilhelm II created a Navy Cabinet separate from the Military Cabinet of the army that had directed the navy. This body's most important task was to transmit all orders on naval affairs in waters near Germany to the appropriate commanders. By the outbreak of World War I, the chief of the Navy Cabinet was Admiral Georg Alexander von Müller, who was viewed by many of the sea commanders as a far more capable administrator than naval officer. Nevertheless, Müller occupied a position of great power as he had direct access to the kaiser. In addition to this organization, Wilhelm created the post of chief of the Admiralty High Command (*Oberkommando*) that was responsible for both strategy and the deployment of warships. Matters pertaining to administration and construction of warships were assigned to the new state secretary of the Imperial Navy Office, which was the post dominated by Tirpitz between 1897 and 1916, when he was forced from office. This navy office was divided into ten departments, each based on the administration of one aspect of the navy, such as shipyards or construction itself. The final change to the administration of the navy occurred in 1899 when Wilhelm II created the Admiralty Staff (*Admiralstab*) to replace the High Command of the navy. This body oversaw, among other things, the strategic planning of the fleet, but in wartime it was also to conduct all naval operations. This body was headed in 1914 by Admiral Hugo von Pohl. The admiral, a career navy man, owed his position in part to the ministrations of Tirpitz, although this support was not based on a respect of his abilities. Indeed, Tirpitz viewed Pohl's value in his being an easily controlled and manipulated subordinate.[62]

The structure of Germany's naval administration was such that no one individual was able to exercise a great deal of power. Rather than being viewed as a weakness, however, the reorganization that provided for this fragmented command had been intended to make sure that the ultimate power rested with the supreme commander of all German naval and military forces: Kaiser Wilhelm II. The kaiser took his role in the imperial government very seriously, and his power in terms of the navy was clearly delineated in Article 53 of the German Constitution of 1871, which served as the governing structure of the unified

Germany. This article stipulated that "The Navy of the Empire is united under the supreme command of the Kaiser. The organization and structure of the same is within the jurisdiction of the Kaiser, who appoints the officers and civil servants of the Navy and receives a direct oath of allegiance."[63] The reorganization served to aid the kaiser in his goal to fully exercise his power.

This intent was oftentimes not realized as the kaiser, despite his belief in the ultimate power of the throne over the navy, was forced to support the wishes of his admirals. Nevertheless, naval officers recognized the system as a hindrance to the conduct of a war. For years prior to the conflict, strategic planning had relied on the consent of the kaiser, and by the outbreak of World War I the actions of the navy were limited in accordance with the kaiser's wishes. This fact is evident through the 1912 fleet orders that restricted offensive operations only to those circumstances deemed as being favorable. This consideration would in theory be made by the kaiser. If the kaiser insisted on his prerogative at the outset of a conflict, chief of the Admiralty Staff Hugo von Pohl would be required to submit all operational plans to the kaiser for imperial approval. By extension, this would limit the actions of commander in chief of the High Seas Fleet Admiral Ingenohl, as he would have to seek approval for any significant operation from Pohl. This administrative machinery consequently posed a great potential hindrance to the actions of the navy in their prosecution of the war. Admiral Reinhard Scheer expounded on the root of this problem in his memoirs: "In view of the peculiarities of naval warfare, the higher authority [meaning the kaiser] cannot be in a position to settle beforehand the details of time and method of any particular enterprise decided upon."[64] Scheer, as well as officers such as Tirpitz, came to believe that the kaiser's insistence on his approval for all operations consigned the navy to inactivity that automatically ceded command of the sea to Britain. This turn of affairs was in part the result of the kaiser's reaction to the Battle of Heligoland Bight.

The cautious nature that the kaiser exhibited at the beginning of the war was not merely the result of an appreciation of Britain's numerical superiority in warships, which had dominated strategic considerations up to the war. One esteemed historian of the German navy asserts that this stance was in part the result of a "psychological impediment" in the sense that the kaiser and all other naval officers were awed by Britain's past naval achievements.[65] This view of a lack of confidence certainly caries a great deal of merit in terms of the kaiser. From the days of his youth, Wilhelm had been taken with the past achievements of the British navy and had dreamed of building a fleet as great as that of Britain.[66] By World War I, the kaiser, the progenitor with Tirpitz of such a navy, was not willing to risk it unnecessarily. This same belief is expressed by others such as Reinhard Scheer, who succinctly summed up the situation: "The English Fleet had the advantage of looking back on a hundred years of proud tradition which must have given every man a sense of superiority based on the great deeds of the past. This could only be strengthened by the sight of their huge fleet, each unit of which in every class was supposed to represent the last word in the art of maritime construction."[67] Not only the kaiser, but also others such as Imperial Chancellor Bethmann-Hollweg, Chief of the Naval Staff von Pohl, and Chief of the Naval Cabinet von Müller agreed with this assessment.

In addition to the psychological factor that lay behind the kaiser's stance were political considerations that reinforced it. Both Wilhelm II and Bethmann-Hollweg viewed the navy as a possibly valuable bargaining chip in negotiations to end a war. In their minds, it was desirable to retain the fleet intact in order to facilitate a favorable conclusion to any European conflict.[68] Although a key consideration in the chancellor's mind was merely to make sure the German coastline was never exposed to British attack, on more than one occasion he used the fleet as a political tool. The kaiser's stance is clear through his continued support of Bethmann-Hollweg until July 1917 despite mounting pressure to dismiss him. It is also clear in the July 1914 war orders to the German fleet that emphasized the steady erosion of British naval might through engagements under purely favorable conditions. So strict was this order that commander in chief of the High Seas Fleet Admiral Ingenohl was not allowed to risk his fleet beyond an imaginary line stretching from Horns Reef to Terschelling in the North Sea.[69] Such a limitation clearly saddled the High Seas Fleet with strictures that made the performance of its duty difficult.

This action was undertaken despite the vigorous opposition of Tirpitz, who was an ardent adversary of Bethmann-Hollweg. The defeat of Tirpitz's position on the matter is indicative of both the power of the kaiser and the course that he was dedicated to pursuing in a naval war. Once Britain declared war on Germany on 4 August 1914, Tirpitz advocated a battle in the area of Heligoland Island, in keeping with the idea of whittling down the British navy's numerical superiority in preparation for a decisive encounter, again somewhere in the region of Heligoland. Aside from the military consideration of defeating the Royal Navy, Tirpitz also had a political motive. He believed that under no circumstance should the fleet remain idle under the strictures imposed by the kaiser. As early as 6 August, Tirpitz was arguing with chief of the Naval Cabinet Müller and Admiral Eduard von Capelle, chief of the Navy Office administration department, that the fleet must assume more rigorous operations. Müller sided with Pohl and the kaiser that the fleet should not be unduly risked.[70]

In sum, the personal rule of the kaiser over the German High Seas Fleet largely crippled what measures were in place for the prosecution of a war with Britain. The restrictions did not allow for the timely seizure of opportunities that presented themselves for large-scale operations. This stricture on command was far more onerous than that imposed on the British navy, and would prove to be a key weakness exacerbated by the Battle of Heligoland Bight.

The problems inherent in the naval high commands of both Britain and

Germany form the last part of the wider backdrop under which the naval war in the North Sea during World War I unfolded. Events leading to the Battle of Heligoland Bight were dictated by the naval arms race, the strategies that arose as a result of it, and the leadership of the individuals within their respective administrations. They also factored heavily into the outcome of the battle and, most importantly in the case of Germany, the ramifications of the contest. The latter signaled ultimately a change in the conduct of the entire naval conflict of World War I.

CHAPTER TWO

NAVAL OPERATIONS UPON THE OUTBREAK OF WORLD WAR I AND THE GENESIS OF THE PLAN FOR A RAID INTO HELIGOLAND BIGHT

A<small>S THE NAVAL ARMS RACE</small> augmented the navies of both Britain and Germany, strategies crystallized for employing the improved fleets in a war between the two nations. While the naval administrations of both countries struggled with how best to pursue operations at sea, events in Europe progressively brought the two powers closer to war. By 1914, Europe was polarized into two different alliance systems, the Triple Alliance and the Triple Entente, in an atmosphere of mutual suspicion. This was partially the result of the alliances themselves. The Triple Alliance members, Germany, the Austro-Hungarian Empire, and Italy, were arrayed against the Triple Entente, Great Britain, France, and Russia. Any conflict in foreign affairs that one member of an alliance might have with a member of the opposite camp invariably involved all members of the respective alliances. As a result, a war between any two members of the respective sides could ultimately result in a war involving all of Europe. This situation was exacerbated by the naval arms race between Britain and Germany. Other sources of friction included an arms race in land forces, imperial competition between the great powers of Europe, and the forces of nationalism. This latter problem, being defined loosely in this case as a general desire by people of a similar cultural background to found their own ethnic state, led to the 28 July 1914 assassination of heir to the Austro-

Hungarian throne Franz Ferdinand by a nationalist Serb society known as the "Black Hand."

While the assassination in itself was not enough to cause a European conflict, the actions of the great powers ultimately produced World War I. Both the Austro-Hungarian Empire and Germany wished to use the assassination to further their own ends in the region of the Balkans. The Austro-Hungarian Empire recognized the event as an opportunity to crush Slavic nationalism, which threatened the integrity of the empire, through a war with Serbia. Germany supported this action in part to retain the support of their primary European ally, but also in the hope of stabilizing the Balkans with the object of establishing firm lines of communication to Turkey. By this time, a Berlin to Baghdad railway constructed for the sake of expanding trade was well on its way to completion and ran through the Balkans.[1] The Germans, as a result, issued the famous "blank cheque," a pledge of support, for the Austro-Hungarian Empire to pursue its goal.

Both German and Austro-Hungarian politicians viewed this as a limited war that would be concluded within a month, but the conflict involved all of the major powers. Two days after Austria-Hungary declared war on Serbia on 28 July 1914, Russia ordered a general mobilization of its military forces. The Russians, who both viewed themselves as the defenders of Slavs and also had ambitions in the Balkans, hoped to force Austria-Hungary to back down. Germany then demanded that Russia cease its mobilization effort. This action was necessary to the Germans as their war plan for a continental war, the Schlieffen Plan, was designed to counter a two-front war versus France and Russia. It relied on a crushing attack against France in order to quickly defeat the country and then a strike against Russia while it was still mobilizing its forces. If Russia mobilized, it would make such a plan impossible to carry out in the event of a European war. As a result of Russian inaction, on 1 August 1914, Germany declared war on Russia. Two days later, a declaration of war was issued to France. By this time, Germany and Austria-Hungary were at war with Russia and France.

This situation, however, did not make war inevitable between Great Britain and Germany. The British vacillated over their decision, and indeed on 26 July King George V of England had expressed his hope that, as Britain had no direct grievance with either Germany or Austria-Hungary, his country would remain neutral.[2] The government of Herbert Asquith largely shared the desire for neutrality in the war. Such was the stance of the British government that the kaiser, his government, and in large part his naval officials believed that Britain would keep out of the war. This hope was shattered on 3 August when the German government sent an ultimatum to Belgium demanding that the German army be allowed to pass freely through it in order to strike at France, in keeping with the Schlieffen Plan. Herbert Asquith's government on 4 August demanded that the Germans respect Belgian neutrality, as Britain had pledged to defend Belgian integrity in an 1839 treaty. To the amazement of the Germans, their decision not to do so led that night to a British declaration of war on Germany.

The opening of hostilities between the two powers initiated the implementation of the opposing sides' strategies. Indeed, both fleets already had been placed on a wartime footing. The British fleet, the core of which was known in the war as the Grand Fleet, was given orders on 28 July to put to sea the following day.[3] By the night of 4 August, the Grand Fleet consisted of twenty dreadnought battleships, five old pre-dreadnought battleships, four battle cruisers, fourteen cruisers of varying types, and forty-one destroyers, under the charge of commander in chief Admiral John Jellicoe. Within these forces, the battle cruisers were under the command of Vice Admiral David Beatty, while six light cruisers were under the charge of Commodore William Goodenough.[4] These were stationed at the principal British naval base of Scapa Flow in the Orkney Islands. Scapa Flow was relatively new, being a consequence of the 1904 reorganization of the fleet in the North Sea, and consequently lacked proper defenses at the outbreak of the war. In addition to the Grand Fleet, to the north were the Sixth and Tenth Cruiser Squadrons, consisting of four and eight cruisers respectively. The Tenth Cruiser Squadron was the force primarily responsible for patrolling the northern entrance to the North Sea in keeping with the strategy of distant blockade adopted by the navy for a war against Germany.

In addition to the forces in the north, there was a collection of naval squadrons in the southern British Isles. The principal force was the Channel Fleet of Vice Admiral Sir Cecil Burney that comprised eighteen older pre-dreadnought battleships and four light cruisers. It was charged with defending the English Channel and protecting transport to and from the continent. In addition was the Harwich Force of Reginald Tyrwhitt. This squadron was situated at the naval base of Harwich on Britain's southeastern coast and comprised two light cruisers and thirty-five destroyers. The Eighth Submarine Flotilla of sixteen submarines and the Sixth Submarine Flotilla of six vessels were also at Harwich under the command of Commodore Roger Keyes. Finally at Harwich was Force C, which consisted of five aging armored cruisers. Assorted lighter forces patrolled the Irish Sea as well as the English Channel.

These forces prepared to meet those of Germany's High Seas Fleet, which received orders on 31 July to move from its base at Kiel in the Baltic through the Kiel Canal to take up their North Sea bases in keeping with the German war plan. On 1 August, the kaiser ordered a general naval mobilization that placed the fleet in readiness for action.[5] At this time, the principal naval bases of the High Seas Fleet were Kiel in the Baltic and Wilhelmshaven and Cuxhaven in the North Sea. Defenses stationed at the outpost of Heligoland guarded the latter two ports, while others guarded the entrance to the Kiel canal that led to the former. From its bases in the North Sea, the High Seas Fleet was under the command of Admiral Friedrich von Ingenohl; it comprised three squadrons.[6]

The First Squadron of eight dreadnought battleships was anchored at the mouth of the Jade River near the large base at Wilhelmshaven. The four dreadnoughts of the Third Squadron lay behind the Jade Bar, a sandy obstruction that lay at the mouth of Jade Bay. This arrangement was in keeping with the kaiser's stressing of fleet protection, particularly in this case against submarine attack. The Second Squadron of eight pre-dreadnought battleships lay at the mouth of the Elbe River between the bases of Cuxhaven and Brunsbüttel. Under the aegis of the High Seas Fleet were also two submarine flotillas comprising nineteen vessels.

Arrayed around the entrances of the Jade, Elbe, and Weser rivers were other forces, many of them charged with guarding these areas and patrolling Heligoland Bight as an advanced outpost for warning the fleet of any major British sortie into the area. Among these were the forces of Germany's Scouting Groups, a collection of battle cruisers, light cruisers, and destroyers (referred to by the Germans as torpedo boats) assigned to five groups. The four battle cruisers of the First Scouting Group under the charge of Rear Admiral Franz Hipper, who as senior officer of the Scouting Groups was stationed at the mouth of the Jade River with the First and Third Squadrons. The other four scouting groups included six light cruisers. The Second Scouting Group was under the command of Hipper's second-in-command, Rear Admiral Leberecht Maas. In addition to this capacity, Maas was also senior officer of torpedo boats. This force consisted of eight torpedo boat flotillas, each consisting normally of eleven vessels, that totaled ninety destroyers. The other force of the German fleet in the area was the Baltic command under Prince Heinrich of Prussia, the kaiser's brother. This force was tasked with the defense against Russian forces and comprised primarily seven cruisers and a collection of torpedo boats, submarines, and minelayers.

Upon the outbreak of war, the British believed that the Germans would use these naval units amassed in the North Sea in one of three operations. One of these was a war on commerce against British shipping in the Atlantic. The second was an invasion of the British east coast, which had been the subject of some planning for a defensive strategy against Germany in the pre-war years. The British believed that the third possibility could be a raid into the English Channel to disrupt operations for transferring the British Expeditionary Force (BEF) to France as part of the continental strategy, which called for the deployment of British ground forces to the continent. In truth, operations were slow to materialize and did not conform to any of the British expectations. The land war on the continent was already unfolding through the German invasion of Belgium, which began on 3 August in order to position the German armies for their assault into France, in keeping with the Schlieffen Plan. In addition, French troops under General Joseph Joffre were massing for an attack from southern France against German forces in the provinces of Alsace and Lorraine. While these events took place, the relative calm in the North Sea belied the notion of war.

Instead of a pitched action to start the war, which most of the British expected, the first naval battle of the conflict was a relatively minor affair. This occurred on 5 August 1914, between British destroyers of the Harwich Force and the German minelayer *Königin Luise*. Built in 1912, this German vessel was a 1,800-ton passenger ship that had served on a line between Hamburg, Germany, and the island of Heligoland, which before the war had been a destination for vacationers. The Germans requisitioned the vessel as a minelayer on the outbreak of war. So quick had been the conversion that most of its peacetime fittings were still in place, the crew was made up largely of the original, peacetime staff, and the weapons consisted merely of two seven-pound pom-pom guns, some rifles, and most importantly 180 mines.[7] The mission of the *Königin Luise* was to lay mines off the port of Harwich while disguised as a vessel that plied the seas between Harwich and the Netherlands. On 5 August, Tyrwhitt was at sea with the Harwich force with the purpose of patrolling in a line from Harwich to the island of Terschelling in Dutch waters. Reports reached him that raised suspicion of the *Königin Luise*'s intentions, and the destroyers *Lance* and *Landrail* were dispatched to investigate. The result was an engagement in which the *Lance* claimed the distinction of firing the first shot of the naval war.[8] The light cruiser *Amphion* soon joined the unequal contest, and the *Königin Luise* was sunk with the loss of some fifty-four officers and men out of its crew of one hundred personnel. Additional action at sea occurred the following day when the *Amphion* was destroyed by a mine laid by the sunken minelayer.

Past these events, operations at sea were quiet. No German interference surfaced against the British operation to transport the British Expeditionary Force to France. This endeavor was approved on 6 August and lasted from 7 August to 22 August. This relatively large-scale operation was a crucial one in terms of shoring up the allied defense of France against German attack. Over this time period, the British transported 160,000 men in six infantry divisions, one cavalry division, two cavalry brigades, and various support units.[9] Throughout the endeavor, not one German vessel sortied to try and disrupt it. Tyrwhitt, whose force was attached to covering the transport of the BEF, in a letter written on 15 August voiced the feeling of the entire Royal Navy, saying that he was beginning to feel "rather bored at looking for nothing" and that he was "beginning to give up hope of getting at the Germans for some time."[10]

The reasons for the lack of a large-scale German naval operation in the opening days of the war, which provoked Tyrwhitt's letter, were many. One of the factors that lay behind the absence of German attacks on the transport of the BEF was the army's belief in a quick end to the war through the success of the Schlieffen Plan. In the minds of the officers in Germany's General Staff, the relatively small BEF would not affect the outcome. General Helmuth von Moltke, the chief of the General Staff, did not view naval interference with the transport of the BEF as important, and even went as far as to say that he hoped that the

British forces would land in time for German troops to "take care of them."[11] Moltke held this view in part because he had long believed that the German Navy could not wrest control of the seas from Britain or, by extension, effectively counter the transport of the BEF to France. His conviction is evident through comments made at a 1909 meeting of government, military, and naval officials where Tirpitz was also present. Moltke, in reaction to a statement by Tirpitz that the navy was not yet strong enough to face the British in a possible conflict, asserted that "I cannot really foresee how this unfortunate situation will ever change, for our navy will always be substantially weaker than the British."[12] This dim view of the navy on the part of the army was strengthened in subsequent talks between the two branches on how best in time of war to actually prevent the BEF from being transported to France. In a 1912 conference between the navy and the army, representative of the navy Admiral von Heeringen advanced the idea of a attack on British forces in the English Channel by the bulk of the German navy.[13] While the High Seas Fleet occupied the majority of the British fleet in a pitched battle, light forces, such as submarines and torpedo boats, would penetrate the area used by the transports. Heeringen, however, admitted that the fleet would be subjected to a numerically superior force in the enemy's home waters. In addition, the admiral saw little chance of success in stopping the transport of British troops. Rather, the best that could be hoped for were small victories that could delay the transport. To this end, the kaiser did approve the use of light forces to harass the transport of the British army. Even so, in the wake of this conference and its unfavorable conclusions, the army concluded that the navy could do little to support the war effort on land.

Aside from the view of the army that resulted from the conclusions reached in the 1912 conference, the German navy itself had its reasons for leaving the British operation unmolested. Playing a role was the navy's estimation, at the 1912 conference, of its own abilities. Heeringen had been forced to admit that an attack by the High Seas Fleet against the British would be contrary to seeking battle under "favorable conditions," the kaiser's order for the use of the fleet that was applied in the 1912 war orders to the navy. It also contradicted the orders to the High Seas Fleet at the outbreak of the conflict that limited major operations to waters that lay to the southeast of a line that ran between Horn's Reef and Terschelling.

Another reason for German inactivity was that German naval officials did not consider the fleet ready for action. Among those who believed this was Admiral Tirpitz, who laid the blame largely at the feet of the German government, particularly the Foreign Office.[14] This assertion has some measure of truth. The High Seas Fleet had undergone battle practice in late July, but afterward the fleet had been distributed to several ports. This was done because the German government, including the kaiser, believed that Britain, the chief potential threat to the High Seas Fleet, would remain neutral in the wake of the Austro-

Hungarian invasion of Serbia. On 26 July, the day after the invasion of Serbia, commander in chief of the High Seas Fleet Admiral Ingenohl had communicated to his officers the German government's belief in Britain's neutral stance. Only on 1 August had the fleet been assembled at Wilhelmshaven. By contrast, the British Royal Navy was ready for action at the outbreak of the conflict after a 10–22 July test mobilization.

Finally, in addition to the German estimation of its naval strength and readiness, the greater issue of strategy dictated operations in the North Sea theater. German pre-war strategy considered that the British might employ either a close or a distant blockade, but the emphasis lay on the former. As a result, the Germans had put into effect the strategy of waiting for the British navy to arrive in the region of the Heligoland Bight to effect its close blockade of the German coasts. Vice Admiral Reinhard Scheer, who at the outbreak of the war was in command of the Second Squadron of the High Seas Fleet, recorded the faith placed in the inevitability of British actions: "There was only one opinion among us, from the Commander-in-Chief down to the latest recruit, about the attitude of the English Fleet. We were convinced that it would seek out and attack our Fleet."[15] This belief, and Germany's strategy overall, proved in error as from the beginning of the war the British instituted a distant blockade, in keeping with their pre-war strategy. As a result, the High Seas Fleet was inactive from the opening of the war.

The war at sea consequently became a waiting game as the two sides prepared for a battle that proved to be out of the question. The German and British strategies that would have assured the battle were based on conditions that did not exist. With the benefit of hindsight, the measures undertaken by the Royal Navy to safeguard the transport of the British Expeditionary Force were unnecessary. The Germans, contrary to the expectations of most British naval officers, did not come through the Heligoland Bight in search of battle. Among those who had expected such a move was Commodore Keyes, who had viewed such an operation as the High Seas Fleet's only recourse.[16]

In the wake of the *Königin Luise*, the German operations that took place in the North Sea were conducted by light forces, in keeping with the restrictions placed on the fleet and the kaiser's willingness to allow use of only such forces rather than the valuable, more powerful warships. These actions were primarily for the sake of reconnaissance. By 6 August, the German naval command was in need of information on both the location of the British fleet and the location of any British blockading force, as neither had presented themselves in the Heligoland Bight as expected. On this date, ten submarines of the First U-Boat Flotilla sortied with orders to search for the British blockade line. Of these ten, one broke down and had to return to port, one (U-13) was lost in unknown circumstances, and a third, U-15, was sunk by the British light cruiser *Birmingham* when the vessel caught the German boat on the surface of the sea and rammed it.[17] Despite the losses, the reconnaissance did provide a somewhat clearer picture of British force dispositions in the North Sea, showing that forces were obviously only in the northern area of the sea.

This allowed Admiral Ingenohl to issue orders for the pursuit of a limited offensive against the British. He was of the mind that, since the reconnaissance revealed British forces only at the northern entrance to the North Sea and in the English Channel, the option open to the fleet was the pursuit of what he termed "guerilla warfare" through raids into the areas of British activity.[18] Despite there being no close blockade, the deployment of light craft was in a sense still in keeping with the original German strategy of steadily eroding British numerical superiority in preparation for a major engagement. Ingenohl attached light cruisers, torpedo boats, submarines, and minelayers to the execution of this operation.

Among these was an operation on the night of 15–16 August, with the sortie of the light cruisers *Köln* and *Stuttgart* with Torpedo Boat Flotillas I and III when they conducted a sweep north-northwest of Heligoland. Their mission was to perform reconnaissance and to engage British submarines thought to be in the area. This sweep proved fruitless, with the exception of the seizure of two neutral Danish merchant vessels transporting food to England. The next major sweep, however, resulted in a clash between German and British naval units that had a direct bearing on the British idea for a raid into Heligoland Bight. On 18 August, the German light cruisers *Stralsund* and *Strassburg*, accompanied by a screen of submarines, steamed into the southern North Sea in search of British forces. Elements of this force encountered patrolling units of the Harwich Force: the light cruiser *Fearless* and sixteen destroyers of the First Flotilla. In the early morning, the British sighted the *Stralsund* and subsequently chased it, but they mistook the German ship for the much heavier cruiser *Yorck*. This gave Captain Wilfred Blunt, the commander of the *Fearless* as well as the First Flotilla, pause. The *Yorck* carried four 210mm guns as well as ten 150mm guns, as opposed to the ten four-inch guns of the *Fearless*. While his flagship and the destroyers certainly outnumbered the Germans, Blunt believed that the advantage that the German vessel enjoyed through the range of its weapons compelled him to call for support. This led to Commodore Tyrwhitt's steaming toward Blunt's position with the remainder of the Harwich Force. In the meantime, Captain Harder of the *Stralsund*, at this point steaming on a course southwest, reversed his course upon information that he was steaming into a trap. By the time the British realized that the ship was the light cruiser *Stralsund* rather than the *Yorck*, the German vessel had gotten away.

Encounters like this could have recurred indefinitely, but the particularly unsatisfactory outcome with the *Stralsund* underlined the general feeling of frustration that existed in Britain over the ploddingly slow nature of the war at sea. In the case of the *Stralsund*, the British had seen their first chance at the action that they had expected since the start of the war, and the opportunity had come to nothing. Commodore Keyes spoke for many in a letter written on 21 August to Admiral Arthur Leveson, the director of the operations division of the Naval War Staff, when he wrote:

> When are we going to make war and make the Germans realize that when-ever they come out—destroyers, cruisers, battleships, or all three—they will be fallen on and attacked?
>
> I feel sick and sore. . . . a light cruiser equal in offensive power to the *Fearless*, has put 16 destroyers and the *Fearless* to flight; however one glosses it over, those are the facts.
>
> Don't think that I am blaming Blunt or his captains. . . . But it is not by such incidents we will get the right atmosphere—for ourselves, absolute confidence and a certain knowledge that "When the enemy come out we will fall on them and smash them," and, on the other side, "When we go out those damned Englanders will fall on us and smash us."
>
> These are the views that I have heard you express—for Heaven's sake preach them![19]

The fact that Keyes mentions Leveson as sharing his views gives insight into the disposition of the one of the chief officials of the Naval War Staff. Indeed, by the time of Keyes letter, the feelings expressed in it weighed heavily as well on First Lord Churchill. They also resonated with the rest of the naval command at sea. Three days after Keyes's letter, Vice Admiral David Beatty, commander of the Grand Fleet's battle cruiser squadron, wrote, "For 30 years I have been waiting for this day [the war] and have as fine a command as one would wish for, and can do nothing. 3 weeks of war and haven't seen the enemy. We shall have to become more offensive."[20]

The same feeling was present in the major ports of the Germany, although the naval command favored patience over a large-scale assault. On 18 August in a meeting with the kaiser, Tirpitz, Pohl, and Müller gave their continued support to pursuing a waiting game, given the British fleet's disposition at the northern entrance of the North Sea rather than in the southern portion for a close blockade. They believed that sooner or later, the British fleet would come into the southern North Sea to seek a decisive battle.[21] Even so, the effect on morale of such a decision was not inconsequential. One regular seaman of the High Seas Fleet commented as early as 5 August that "[e]verything is the same as it used to be. The monotony has a depressing effect. Expressions of disgust at our inactivity are heard everywhere."[22] Few individuals on either side of the naval war was satisfied with the state of affairs in the war at sea.

On the British side, the inaction was most keenly felt by the leaders of those forces involved in the few, fleeting actions there had been through the 18 August engagement, or lack thereof, with the *Stralsund*. The episode with the *Stralsund* served as the catalyst for action on the part of the leaders of forces in the base of Harwich. Chief among these was Commodore Roger Keyes. Born in 1872, Keyes had entered the navy as a cadet in 1885 and attained the rank of lieutenant eight years later. He gained the reputation of being a capable and particularly aggressive commander through his actions in the 1900–1901 Boxer Rebellion in China. Following his promotion to captain in 1905, Keyes was regarded as one of the navy's most promising officers. Through subsequent experience with submarines, in 1912 Keyes was appointed commodore of the Royal Navy's submarine service. By 1914, Keyes found himself the senior naval officer at the port of Harwich. As a consequence of his position, he also maintained an office in the Admiralty in London and had direct access to chief of the Naval War Staff Admiral Doveton Sturdee. Upon the British ultimatum to Germany on 4 August, the commodore exhibited the zeal for offensive action that had helped him succeed in the service: he gave a speech to the men of his force that so energized them that it met with thunderous cheering.[23] Such a spirit, as is evidenced by the letter of 21 August, reacted poorly to inaction. Upon the outbreak of the conflict, Keyes's force comprised some of the newest submarines in the fleet and the destroyers *Lurcher* and *Firedrake*, which acted as leaders for the submarines.

The commodore was not alone in his aggressive drive for action in the war at sea. The commodore's force shared its base of Harwich with two other independent commands. One of these, the Shotley Training Establishment for boys under the command of Captain Cuthbert Cayley, had little bearing on the war; the other, the Harwich Force, was commanded by Keyes's colleague Commodore Reginald Tyrwhitt. Born in 1870, Tyrwhitt entered the navy as a cadet in 1883 and by 1892 was promoted to lieutenant. In 1896, he took command of one of the first destroyers of the Royal Navy, which began his long career involving this type of warship. By 1914, Tyrwhitt's expertise had earned him his appointment in charge of the Harwich Force, comprising the thirty-five destroyers of the First and Third Flotillas as well as the light cruisers *Fearless* and *Amphion*. The *Fearless* acted as the leader of the First Flotilla, while the *Amphion* had charge of the Third Flotilla. Tyrwhitt's flagship was the aging light cruiser *Amethyst*, which he characterized as being too slow for operations with the destroyers and other cruisers. This estimation was quite correct, as the top speed of the flagship was 22.5 knots. Both *Fearless* and *Amphion* were capable of 25 knots, while many of the destroyers could achieve 29 knots.[24] This problem was exacerbated by the loss of the *Amphion* as the *Amethyst* was more often employed in its place.

These two commanders efficiently used the forces at their disposal in an atmosphere where the two commands were on good terms with one another. Keyes and Tyrwhitt enjoyed a good relationship with one another as both professionals and friends. Both were offensive-minded, and their forces had conducted joint exercises together over the course of the year before the outbreak of the conflict. A meeting between Keyes and Tyrwhitt on 1 August led them both to write letters to their wives in which each expressed his professional admiration and friendship for the other. Keyes wrote about Tyrwhitt and the Harwich force that "he [Tyrwhitt] and the destroyer flotilla have a great respect for the submarines—and we are working together—I am glad to think that Tyrwhitt is the Commodore. He is a splendid fellow and we are such very good friends."[25] Tyrwhitt in his letter records much the same. He wrote that "Roger and I get on well and he is a great comfort to me, as he approves of my arrangements and I of his. Perhaps we are a mutual admiration society, which is just as well as we have much in common just now."[26] As a result of this relationship, not only were Keyes's submarine forces and Tyrwhitt's Harwich Force used to joint operations, collectively making them a far more effective fighting force, but also the two commanders knew the other's mind, which proved a potentially great advantage in battle.

The orders for the use of the forces under Keyes's and Tyrwhitt's command were based on guarding against the presumed attack of German forces that would ensue on the outbreak of war. Keyes's orders were to use his submarines to patrol the Jade and Weser Rivers of Germany not only for reconnaissance, but also to attack any German naval units that might leave their bases for the operations that the British had expected to unfold at the opening of the war. Tyrwhitt's forces were to patrol the eastern portion of the English Channel in the area between 52 degrees and 54 degrees north latitude. This area encompassed the waters between Harwich and Flamborough Head, just south of the city of Scarborough on England's east coast. Tyrwhitt's mission was to guard against minelayers, such as the *Königin Luise*, protect against raids into the channel by German forces, and support the Channel Fleet.

Keyes and Tyrwhitt executed their orders on the outbreak of war in an atmosphere that allowed them a fair degree of independence from higher authority. As of 10 August, technically both Keyes and Tyrwhitt were under the command of Rear Admiral Arthur Henry Christian, who was in command of Cruiser Force C (also known as the Seventh Cruiser Squadron). Christian flew his flag in the aging *Bacchante*-class cruiser *Euryalus* and oversaw his other five old cruisers and the rest of the forces at Harwich, known collectively as the Southern Force. Even so, Christian was not a very able leader, which allowed Keyes and Tyrwhitt to seize the initiative themselves.

The lack of offensive action in the war at sea on the part of the Grand Fleet proved quickly galling, but greatly magnifying both men's restlessness was that they too enjoyed little concrete success in the opening days of the war. The German fleet simply did not sortie, for reasons previously discussed. Engagements like the *Königin Luise* were fleeting. More commonplace than this kind of battle were monotonous patrols. On 5–7 August, Tyrwhitt and some of Keyes submarines steamed out of Harwich, to the cheers of three hundred boys between the ages of fourteen and fifteen from the Shotley Barracks, to a point thirty miles from Borkum that lay at the mouth of the Ems River of Germany — but saw no action. During the transport of the BEF to France, Tyrwhitt's forces maintained a patrol on a line generally from Heligoland southeast to the mouth of the Ems River, and then south-southeast to Terschelling. This too came to naught, and it is not surprising therefore that the failed incident with the *Stralsund* had prompted such a response from Keyes as is found in his 21 August letter. Tyrwhitt echoed that sentiment following an operation 20–22 August where some of Admiral Christian's Force C and destroyers of the Harwich Force patrolled off the coast of Ostend, Belgium. The Naval War Staff had called for this show of force to try to at least delay the Germans' capture of the port of Ostend, as the British believed that Germany could use the port as a staging point for strikes against the lines of supply through the English Channel from England to the BEF in France. This operation, like most of the others, led to no offensive action. On the verge of retiring from the operations area on 22 August, Tyrwhitt was of the same mind as Keyes in his letter of the day before. In a letter to his wife, Tyrwhitt vented his frustration: "I have been here [Ostend] two days and feel like a madman. . . . However I am off in two hours and I hope I shall not have to come back again for ages."[27]

Tyrwhitt's writing proved true in the sense that he would not be on an uneventful, extended patrol again for a while. In Tyrwhitt's absence, Keyes had formulated a plan (in keeping with the sentiments aired in his letter to Leveson) that had the object of placing the Royal Navy on the offensive in the North Sea. It was based on information that Keyes had garnered through his submarines' reconnaissance into Heligoland Bight. The first of these reconnaissance missions occurred three hours after the outbreak of the war when Keyes dispatched *E-6* and *E-8* of the Eighth Submarine Flotilla to Heligoland Bight. Although the Germans did detect these vessels, neither one was attacked, and each returned with useful information on the disposition of German forces defending the bight. Keyes garnered further intelligence through a reconnaissance sweep into the bight on 19–20 August that he conducted himself and a sortie on 23 August of submarines *E-4*, *E-9*, and *D-5*. This latter reconnaissance group garnered their information at great risk, as they were hunted by German destroyers in the area. Thanks to these operations, Keyes was able to describe the strategic situation in Heligoland Bight, during both the night and the day, in some detail. Up to 15 August, the area had been occupied by seemingly hundreds of German, Danish, and Dutch fishing trawlers and small merchant vessels; the Germans left the bight open to civilian traffic in the opening days of the war.[28] Aside from these, the Germans were clearly executing an organized patrol around the island of Heligoland. Keyes laid out his intelligence data in a letter for chief of the Naval War Staff Sturdee: "A very large number of destroyers are employed in the daytime North and South of Heligoland, apparently with the object of preventing mine laying and harassing submarines. . . . At about 5.0 or 6.0 p.m. the destroyers detailed for night work appear to be led to certain points by light cruisers. They then 'fan out' and proceed to sea at a good speed—returning at daylight."[29]

This information proved correct in general terms, although the composition and operation of the force changed frequently over the first weeks of the war. Soon after the beginning of the conflict, the Germans believing that the British fleet would quickly descend on the German coast, had put into place observation patrols in Heligoland Bight. These forces were in place to warn of such a sortie and also to defend the entrances to Germany's major ports against mine-layers and submarines. On 1 August, the task of observing the bight fell to Rear Admiral Franz Hipper, the senior officer of the Scouting Forces. Hipper was born in 1863 and graduated from the German Naval Academy in 1884; his naval experience rested with cruisers and to a lesser degree torpedo boats, which accounted in part for his initial wartime appointment. Commander in chief of the High Seas Fleet Admiral Ingenohl described Hipper in May 1914 as being "[e]nergetic, fresh, tenacious and progressing in an outstanding manner in the scouting service."[30] With the support of his commander in chief, on 5 August Hipper set up two patrol lines in the bight, each maintained by a torpedo boat flotilla, meaning eleven craft each. The outer line patrolled an arc of a radius of thirty-five miles, while the inner spanned twenty-three miles from the lightship Elbe I that lay at the mouth of the Elbe River. A distance of twelve miles lay between these two arcs. Between these two lines of torpedo boats was a third line, comprising submarines, on an arc of twenty-nine miles radius. One light cruiser each was stationed at both the northern and the southern ends of the patrol lines, while a third was stationed at Heligoland.[31] In addition to these forces, another light cruiser and a torpedo boat flotilla lay at the mouth of the Weser River in order to respond promptly to a British attack in the bight. During the night, the outermost patrol as well as the submarines patrol retired to their North Sea bases, leaving only the inner line active. In the early morning, these two lines were reestablished.

Hipper quickly revised this scheme due to protests from some of his submarine commanders, beginning on 6 August, who pointed out that the maintenance of such a patrol placed great strain on the machinery of the vessels in the defense. Indeed, all forces of the patrol suffered this problem, as they were all lightly built craft that were not designed for the continuous operation that Hipper's plan demanded. Consequently, Hipper dispensed with the line of submarines. A day after the protests that sparked this change, the rear admiral withdrew the innermost patrol line of torpedo boats for the sake of not wearing out their machinery. In order to address the lack of the inner and middle lines of defense, the remaining forces of the outer arc now patrolled in an area between the two original destroyer patrols. Finally, the forces on standby at the Weser were also detached from duty. Interestingly, the Germans considered as an ultimate solution to the wear placed on their ships the laying of a minefield in the Heligoland Bight. Ingenohl, however, as well as other naval officials, stood against this plan. In their minds, such a minefield would hamper the operations of the German fleet, particularly given the fact that the high command still envisioned a British attack in the region of Heligoland Bight as they executed a close blockade.[32] Had the Germans executed this plan, the Battle of Heligoland Bight would never have occurred as it did.

Hipper recognized that the defense in place was lacking in the sense that few forces protected the bight under his new plan. The rear admiral addressed this problem with a new scheme of defense that called on the torpedo boats of the outer patrol to cruise in the area of their original arc at a distance of between three and four miles apart during daytime. Hipper added an inner line of mine-sweepers—a collection of aging torpedo boats—and held an additional destroyer flotilla in readiness for immediate action. At night, the torpedo boats retired to an arc of twenty-five miles, while the disposition of the cruisers remained the same. An additional cruiser was also dispatched to Heligoland during the night hours.

This defense, despite Hipper's best efforts, suffered from several weaknesses that hampered the defense of the bight. One of these concerned the division of command in the German navy. Although Ingenohl appointed Hipper to over-see the defense of the bight, it was the commander in chief who issued the first orders for defensive positions in the region of Heligoland. The inadequacy of these measures had forced Hipper to restructure the system. Even so, each successive plan proved to be of only limited value because the disposition of the patrolling craft did not allow for them to support one another against a British raid into the bight. This problem resulted largely from Ingenohl's continued interference in the affairs of his subordinate: "It was characteristic of Admiral von Ingenohl that although he placed the security of Helgoland [sic] Bay under the Commander of the Scouting Forces, he then proceeded to give detailed orders as to how the light cruisers, torpedo boats, minesweepers, and submarines should operate."[33] The set patrolling areas in Ingenohl's orders allowed for a situation where the patrolling vessels could be isolated and destroyed piecemeal, making an effective defense of the bight difficult if not impossible. Exacerbating this problem was the fact that there were few ships on the patrol in general—it was at most a torpedo boat flotilla—and they were responsible for a huge radius of patrol that spanned the entire bight.

An additional weakness lay in the lack of heavy support for the vessels of the patrol. This problem resulted from the fact that the Germans could not maintain a constant readiness for action from their North Sea bases. At the outbreak of war, none of the North Sea bases possessed adequate defenses, such as submarine nets, to guard against the attack of enemy submersibles. Indeed, these would not be available for the first six months of the war. In terms of the major naval base at Wilhelmshaven, the Germans first allowed units of the High Seas

Fleet to anchor in the outer Jade during the day, provided that each ship deployed their own torpedo nets; at night the ships were withdrawn to Schillig Roads, the stretch of water that lay at the entrance to the port of Wilhelmshaven. Through this procedure, the Germans at night took advantage of the one significant defense against submarines at their disposal: the Jade Bar that proved difficult for submerged submarines to pass. This practice changed on 7 August with the detection of British submarines in the area of the bight; these happened to be those of Commodore Keyes's reconnaissance group. As a result, almost all of the heavy units of the High Seas Fleet were ordered to stay always behind the Jade Bar. The problem with this procedure was that, in the event of a British attack in the bight, the larger vessels, such as battleships and battle cruisers, would have to wait until early afternoon for the tide to rise to a point where the vessels could cross the Jade Bar without grounding. By that time, a battle that had started in the early morning could be over. In this situation, the only heavy unit available was the ship posted for patrol duty at the fortified island of Wangerooge, which lay near the entrance to Wilhelmshaven. At the time of the Battle of Heligoland Bight, this vessel was the powerful dreadnought battleship *Helgoland*, but one such vessel unsupported in a battle would run considerable risks from submarines and light craft. The only vessels consequently available to the patrols of the bight in case of an attack were lighter craft, comprising cruisers, destroyers, submarines, and steam trawlers, that patrolled the Jade and Weser Rivers. The latter craft were far too small and in many cases too old for a modern naval battle.

Keyes and the British in general would benefit from these weaknesses, as Keyes's intelligence data formed one part of a larger letter written on 23 August for submission to Sturdee that detailed a plan to attack the German forces guarding Heligoland Bight. Keyes proposed that his submarines attack the forces in the bight at a point when, according to his information, the Germans were relieving the patrol on station with a fresh group of torpedo boats. Under this scheme, the British submarines would sortie at night to a point off the coast of Germany and lie there submerged on the sea floor, for the purposes of conserving battery power, until the hours just before dawn, when they would be met by destroyers of the Harwich Force. At this time, the destroyers and submarines would conduct a sweep into the bight in order to catch the German destroyers of the patrols as they steamed back to their ports. Keyes believed that this operation could "inflict considerable loss on these destroyer patrols."[34] On the same day that Keyes penned his proposal, he had the opportunity to share it with Tyrwhitt, who had returned from his unsatisfactory duty off the coast of Ostend. Keyes intoned that he was going to use his access to the Naval War Staff that his station provided and present the plan personally to the Admiralty. Tyrwhitt, given his shared predisposition for offensive operations with Keyes, enthusiastically backed the plan and authorized Keyes to speak on his behalf in support of the scheme.

At first, Keyes did not meet with success upon his arrival at the Admiralty. The members of the Naval War Staff seemed far too ensconced in the daily minutia of running the war at sea to give the commodore an audience. Undeterred, Keyes was able to get a message to First Lord Churchill stating that he was at the Admiralty, should the first lord wish to see him. Churchill received Keyes, which allowed the spirited commodore "the opportunity of bursting into flame about it, which fired the First Lord."[35] That Churchill would be receptive was not a surprise. The idea of a raid into Heligoland Bight was certainly not a new one.

By the time Keyes arrived at the Admiralty with his plan of attack, there had been multiple plans to assault German forces in the bight. The progenitor of one of them was Churchill himself. In the days after the outbreak of the war, the lack of offensive actions had weighed heavily not only on such individuals as Keyes and Tyrwhitt, but also on the first lord. On 12 August, Churchill directed Captain Herbert Richmond, the assistant director of the Operations Division of the Naval War Staff, to work with Admiral Christian, the commander of the Southern Force, toward a plan to raid Heligoland Bight. The first lord envisioned it primarily as a destroyer operation in which one flotilla, presumably of the Harwich Force, some submarines, again presumably of Keyes's flotillas, and the *Bacchante*-class cruisers of Christian's Cruiser Force C would take part. Richmond himself was quite averse to the plan and believed it to be "an amateur piece of work of a medieval type."[36] The operation, however, was never executed; on 14 August, with the plans prepared, Admiral Christian was informed by the Naval War Staff that the decision had been made to cancel it. Even so, the idea of such a plan did not vanish with the shelving of Churchill's scheme. Churchill dreamt of even invading and occupying Heligoland, in keeping with former first sea lord Admiral Arthur Wilson's plans.[37] Of a more concrete nature, however, was a scheme presented on 18 August by commander in chief of the Grand Fleet Admiral Jellicoe. He proposed a much more audacious plan than Churchill's for a raid into Heligoland Bight—a plan that relied on cooperation between the Grand Fleet and Admiral Christian's Southern Force. He called for a sweep to within thirty miles of Heligoland with both flotillas of the Harwich Force, covered by cruisers and submarines. In addition, the Grand Fleet would sortie in support of the principal forces of the raid. Jellicoe slated 23 August for a rendezvous of these forces at sea, with operations beginning the following day.[38] Jellicoe believed that this operation had a good chance of catching major units of the High Seas Fleet at sea. At the time of the planning, the BEF was in the process of being transported to France, and Jellicoe believed that there was the possibility that German units might be at sea to disrupt the operation. As with Churchill's plan, this scheme did not come to fruition. The Naval War Staff, although it looked favorably on the plan, postponed it due to the need for retaining the Harwich Force and that of Keyes to guard the crossing of a division of the British Expeditionary Force. This stymied the potential sortie, as the forces Jellicoe needed were available only at the close of the operation to transport the British troops to France. In the mind of the commander in chief, the opportunity to catch the High Seas Fleet at sea had passed.[39]

The stillbirth of both of these plans, however, had not quelled the first lord's desire for such an endeavor. Upon hearing of Keyes's plan, Churchill called a meeting, set for 24 August, to discuss it in detail with other members of the Admiralty. He also directed that Tyrwhitt should attend the meeting, which caused no small problem for the commodore. When Tyrwhitt received the order by wireless at 9:30 A.M. on the scheduled day of the meeting, he was one hundred miles out from Harwich conducting a patrol with the First Flotilla. Even through using his fastest destroyer, the commodore did not arrive at the Admiralty until 5:00 in the afternoon. Waiting for him were First Lord Churchill, chief of the Naval Staff Sturdee, first sea lord Prince Louis of Battenberg, and second sea lord Vice Admiral Sir Frederick Hamilton.

Over the course of the evening, the assembled officers and officials discussed the plan and slightly modified it, in part due to Sturdee's concerns. He believed that an inshore operation ran the risk of the Harwich Force potentially facing two flotillas of enemy torpedo boats: one steaming back to port from its night patrol and the other steaming to its defensive position.[40] The idea of an inshore operation with a sweep outward into the bight to catch vessels returning from patrol was scrapped in favor of an opposite approach. There was general agreement that the thrust of the sweep would take place beginning to the northwest of Heligoland so as to intercept the German day patrol of submarines. Keyes would split his submarines into three forces. One group would occupy a position off the coast of Germany near the Ems River to catch any large German warships that might sortie from their bases on the outbreak of battle. Another group would place itself some forty miles from the Elbe lightship to the north of Heligoland. Their mission was to make themselves visible to German warships and thus lure them in chase farther out to sea and into the approaching Harwich Force. The latter had orders to steam to a position twenty-five miles southwest of Horns Reef light by 4:00 A.M. before proceeding south for four hours to a position twelve miles west of Heligoland. This maneuver would place the British force behind the Germans' patrol line and thus cut the vessels off from their bases at Heligoland and on the North Sea coast. At this point, around 8:00 A.M., the force would turn westward and attack the forces of the German patrols in the rear. Based on Keyes's intelligence reports, it appeared that the day patrol of destroyers would be well out to sea and thus vulnerable. If Keyes's submarines were successful, the situation of the Germans would be even more favorable for the British to inflict losses on them. The final force of submarines would occupy a position off the northern and southern coasts of Heligoland to attack any cruisers that might sortie to the aid of the German torpedo boats.[41]

All agreed on the types of warships that Tyrwhitt and Keyes should employ in order to execute the plan. Tyrwhitt's force comprised the entire Harwich Force, the core of which was the First and Third Flotillas of thirty-one destroyers. Each of these flotillas comprised four divisions. The First Flotilla was not at its normal full strength. It counted fifteen craft rather nineteen, as the Admiralty detached a division to support battle cruisers stationed at the Humber River. The Third Flotilla comprised sixteen destroyers. The two light cruisers of the force acted as the leaders of the flotillas. The light cruiser *Fearless* was commanded by Captain Wilfred Blunt, who would command the First Flotilla. The Third Flotilla fell to Tyrwhitt, who received as his flagship the light cruiser *Arethusa*, which was a brand new vessel. Keyes's force comprised eight submarines. Three each were earmarked for duty as the outer line of submarines (acting as a lure) and as the force near Heligoland. The last two were the ships intended for the mouth of the Ems River. Leading these ships and stationed near the decoy force would be two destroyers: Keyes's flagship *Lurcher* and the *Firedrake*.

With the plan and the core of the raiding force generally agreed upon, the source of contention in the meeting became supporting units for the operation. The individuals in the meeting generally agreed to the use of the battle cruisers *Invincible* and *New Zealand*, stationed at the Humber. These vessels, under the command of Rear Admiral Archibald Moore, would cruise to the northwest of Tyrwhitt and Keyes in case heavy support was necessary against any German warships that might sortie to aid the Heliogland Bight patrol. The inclusion, however, of Rear Admiral Christian's Seventh Cruiser Squadron had to be a source of consternation for both Keyes and Tyrwhitt. As overall commander of the Southern Force, Christian technically had command of the operation, and members of the committee probably believed that his forces should be used accordingly. Even so, all of the ships of this force—six of them, including Tyrwhitt's old flagship, the *Amethyst*, as an attached vessel for the operation—were far too old to be of much use at all. The orders for the force placed them in reserve off Terschelling in order to intercept any German vessels that might be chased into the area by Tyrwhitt's sweep, but they were so slow that Christian's command would be able to do little to hunt down such craft.[42] Keyes had made his feelings about Christian's force known in his 21 August letter to Admiral Leveson: "For Heaven's sake take those 'Bacchantes' [referring to the name of the ship class of the cruisers in Force C] away. . . . Goodness knows there is no reflection on the gallant fellows in them! I don't say those cruisers will be attacked, but the Germans must know they are about, and if they send out a suitable force, God help them."[43] These words proved prophetic. On 22 September 1914, one German submarine sank the *Cressy*, the *Hogue*, and the *Aboukir* of this force.

Keyes, in the desire to have more supporting units of worth, consequently suggested that the six light cruisers of the First Light Cruiser Squadron, under the command of Commodore William Goodenough, should take part in the operation. In addition, Keyes also made a case for the inclusion of Vice Admiral David Beatty's First Battle Cruiser Squadron. Keyes simply did not believe that there was sufficient supporting strength provided to guard against a concerted attack by German forces defending the patrol. The request for more supporting units, however, did not lead to the assent of the members of the Admiralty. Sturdee simply replied that no units of the Grand Fleet, of which all of the requested units were a part, would be available for the operation. This reaction proved indicative of Sturdee's belief that the Grand Fleet needed all of its force for use at any time. Keyes's request was not the first time that Sturdee had rejected such a proposal. During the earlier planning for a raid into Heligoland Bight, from 12–14 August, Sturdee stymied the request from Captain Richmond and Admiral Christian for use of the First Light Cruiser Squadron.[44] Despite the rebuff of Keyes's request, both he and Tyrwhitt accepted the lack of supporting units. Both were eager for approval of the plan, in keeping with their desire for offensive action in the war at sea. Upon the settlement of this question, the members of the Admiralty accepted the plan and set operations to begin on 26 August with the sortie of the forces for the raid. The Admiralty members, Keyes, and Tyrwhitt, began to draw up orders accordingly.

The question of supporting units, however, did not end with the meeting. From the start, the weaknesses in the administrative organization of the Admiralty hampered the operation and produced a potentially disastrous situation for Keyes and Tyrwhitt. Both commodores informed their ship commanders that the only British warships in Heligoland Bight larger than a destroyer would be Tyrwhitt's light cruisers. Keyes and Tyrwhitt instructed their commanders that any other heavy unit sighted should be considered as hostile. Events that transpired in the war on the European continent, however, led to the Admiralty's last-minute inclusion of additional warships for support of the operation, which undermined Keyes and Tyrwhitt's orders. Changing conditions had greatly increased the importance of the raid in the overall course of the war. On 25 August, the decision was made to transport three thousand Royal Marines to Ostend, Belgium, to defend the Belgian coast against advancing units of the German army in the region. As a result, in First Lord Churchill's thinking, the operation into the bight became more than just a raid. Churchill now believed that the raid could serve as a diversion against a potential sortie of major units of the German High Seas Fleet in response to the movement of the marines. The first lord consequently contacted commander in chief of the Grand Fleet Jellicoe to inform him not only of the raid into the bight, but also of the chance that major units of the German fleet might put to sea.

This would not have been a problem but for the fact that there was little coordination of the plan for the raid into Heligoland Bight due to poor communication within the Admiralty and particularly the Naval War Staff. Indeed, there was poor communication between the Admiralty and the navy itself overall, which was a chief criticism of it in the first years of the war. Jellicoe did not learn of the operation into Heligoland Bight until 26 August, the same day earmarked for forces of the raid to sortie, when he received a message from the Admiralty that read, "A destroyer sweep of First and Third Flotillas with submarines suitably placed is in orders for Friday from east to west, commencing between Horn Reef and Heligoland, with battle cruisers in support."[45] This extremely tardy communiqué alarmed Jellicoe, as he believed that this force did not have the support necessary to ward off an attack by heavy German warships. His belief in the need for such support was evident in his earlier plans for a raid into Heligoland Bight, when he advocated the use of the bulk of the Grand Fleet. In the wake of the Admiralty's cryptic message, Jellicoe asked for more information and "made urgent representations as to the necessity of supporting the force."[46] His first message reflects some of the anxiety that the admiral felt. Two hours after the original message, Jellicoe wired the Admiralty with a proposal to "co-operate in sweep on Friday (28th), moving Grand Fleet Cruisers and Destroyers to suitable positions with Battle Fleet near. Request that I be given full details of proposed operations."[47] The admiral received precious little in response to his call for more information. Ultimately, Jellicoe was not sure who was in command of the operation, although he did know that the Harwich Force and submarines were taking part. By inference, the admiral could guess that Admiral Christian as well as Commodores Keyes and Tyrwhitt were involved. Even so, he was not given concrete details of the direction of the sweep, its starting point, or the ships taking part in the raid. Only just after midnight on 27 August did the Admiralty finally transmit that "co-operation by battle fleet not required. Battle cruisers can support if convenient."[48] The Naval War Staff allowed for the use of the battle cruisers due to the need for at least some measure of support to strengthen the raid in the wake of its increased importance in protecting the amphibious operation to Ostend. Jellicoe immediately took steps in keeping with the Admiralty telegram, although he went beyond its limits to include the dispatch of not only Beatty's First Battle Cruiser Squadron, but also Commodore Goodenough's light cruisers.

This measure, although designed to help, could have doomed the operation. For Jellicoe, the tardiness of the Admiralty in briefing him on the raid led to the dispatch of vessels at the last minute for them to be useful as support. This fact combined with further poor communication from the Admiralty led to a situation where neither Tyrwhitt or Keyes received any information that more heavy British units would be supporting the raid. Given the orders to the commanders in Tyrwhitt's and Keyes's forces, an encounter between these units and those of the raid presented the chance that the Royal Navy might lose valuable units of the fleet to fire from its own forces. Nevertheless, all by this time was in place. The Battle of Heligoland Bight, the first naval engagement between the forces of the British Royal Navy and the German navy, was about to begin.

CHAPTER THREE

THE COMMENCEMENT OF THE BATTLE OF HELIGOLAND BIGHT

As the strategic purpose of the raid and its force strength changed, the myriad forces of the operation prepared to make steam for their positions in the North Sea. The force overall included some of the newest and most powerful units of the British Navy. The first units to leave their base were those under the command of Commodore Keyes. At midnight on 26 August, the destroyer leaders *Lurcher*, Keyes's flagship, and *Firedrake* put to sea with the submarines *D-2*, *D-8*, *E-4*, *E-5*, *E-6*, *E-7*, *E-8*, and *E-9*.[1] Both the destroyer leaders, launched in 1912, belonged to the *Acheron*-class. The hull of such a vessel measured 246'×25' 6"×9' and displaced 778 tons. The armament of each consisted of two 4-inch guns, one each being placed fore and aft, two 12-pound guns, and two 21-inch torpedo tubes. Being destroyers, they possessed no armor but high speed, being a maximum of 32 knots. Of the submarines, the least capable were *D-2* and *D-8* of the *D*-class. Approved in 1906, *D-2* measured 162' 1"×10' 9½" (when surfaced) and displaced 489 tons on the surface of the sea. Its sister ship, *D-8*, measured 164' 7"×11' 5" (surfaced) and displaced 495 tons when surfaced. The armament of both vessels consisted of three 18-inch torpedo tubes, two in the bow and one in the stern, and one 12-pound deck gun. Their machinery generated a maximum speed of 14 knots on the surface and 9 knots submerged. The submarines *E-4*, *E-5*, *E-6*, *E-7*, and *E-8*

Sicherung in der Deutschen Bucht
am Morgen des 28. VIII. 1914.

Fig. 1. Heligoland Bight

measured 178' 1"×22' 8⅜"×12' 6¼" and displaced 655 tons when surfaced. The ship mounted four 18-inch torpedo tubes, one each being placed in the bow and stern and two in the sides of the hull, and one 12-pound deck gun. Its machinery allowed for 15 knots on the surface and 9 knots submerged. Submarine *E-9* was generally similar to these, being only slightly larger and mounting an additional torpedo tube in the bow. Keyes, with the *Lurcher* and *Firedrake*, was set to steam to a location north of Heligoland with submarines *E-6*, *E-7*, and *E-8*, which would serve as the decoy ships to lure German forces farther into the North Sea. Submarines *E-4*, *E-5*, and *E-9* served as the inner force

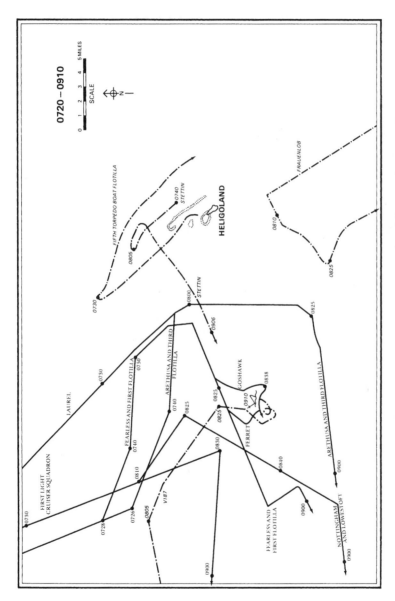

0720 – 0910

SCALE

0 1 2 3 4 5 MILES

N

FIFTH TORPEDO BOAT FLOTILLA

0730

0805

0740
STETTIN

HELIGOLAND

0810

0825

FRAUENLOB

0800
STETTIN

0906

0730

LAUREL

FIRST LIGHT
CRUISER SQUADRON

0730

ARETHUSA AND THIRD
FLOTILLA

FEARLESS AND FIRST FLOTILLA

0750

0740

0740

0825

0730

0728

0810

0805

V.187

0830

0825
0825

0838
GOSHAWK

0910

FERRET

0840

0825

ARETHUSA AND THIRD FLOTILLA

0900

0805

0900

FEARLESS AND
FIRST FLOTILLA

0900

0900

NOTTINGHAM
AND LOWESTOFT

Fig. 2. Phase 1. *Reproduced through the kind permission of the Naval Institute Press.*

around the island of Heligoland, while D-2 and D-8 possessed orders to lie in wait off the Ems River as according to the plan.

Following Keyes were the light cruisers and destroyers of the Harwich Force under Commodore Tyrwhitt. This force sortied at 5:00 A.M. on 27 August, the only exception being Captain Wilfred Blunt in the light cruiser *Fearless*, which joined the rest of the force at sea that afternoon.[2] Of the two light cruisers that led the two destroyer flotillas, Tyrwhitt's flagship, the *Arethusa*, represented the cutting edge of British technological development in vessels of its type. Completed in August 1914 and given to Tyrwhitt expressly for the Heligoland Bight raid, the *Arethusa* had features that made it an impressive ship. The hull measured 436'×39'×13' 5" and displaced 3,750 tons. Its armament consisted of two 6-inch guns, six 4-inch weapons, one 3-pound gun, and four 21-inch torpedo tubes. This ship carried armor protection in the form of a belt that varied between three inches and one inch in thickness as well as an armored deck one inch deep. The machinery of the *Arethusa* was capable in theory of a maximum speed of 28½ knots.[3] Tyrwhitt was thrilled to get the new vessel. He was in a situation where he had gone from the "oldest and slowest [the *Amethyst*] to the newest and fastest light cruiser," but the condition of *Arethusa* was such that it gave Tyrwhitt pause concerning its potential performance in the operation.[4] The vessel was commissioned only fifteen days before the operation, and the commodore did not receive the ship until 9:00 A.M. on 26 August, in the midst of final preparations to steam into battle. There was precious little time to test the ship and its untrained crew. The experience Tyrwhitt did glean upon immediately taking the ship to sea for gunnery practice did not inspire confidence. The vessel's highest speed in trials was only 25 knots, and the 4-inch guns frequently jammed when fired as a result of an apparent defect in the cartridge ejectors that cleared the spent shell casings from the weapons. This problem was so frequent that Tyrwhitt ordered firing of them discontinued in the exercise. Tyrwhitt summed up his problems in a letter to his brother on the day of the test firing: "I am of course delighted at getting such a splendid new ship, but it is rather a trial having a new ship's company and new guns. . . . I expect we shall soon get it in order, but I would like to have had a week to do it in."[5] Tyrwhitt had only hours to work with rather than the several days that he had hoped for. This problem made itself felt in the coming battle and to an extent hampered the operation overall.

The other ships of the Harwich Force were seasoned vessels with trained crews. Captain Blunt's *Fearless* was older than *Arethusa*, but given the latter's condition the difference was negligible in terms of fighting power. The *Fearless*, completed in 1913, measured 406'×41' 6"×15' 7" and displaced 3,440 tons. It carried ten 4-inch guns in single mounts, four 3-pound weapons, and two 18-inch torpedo tubes. This ship possessed minimal armor protection, just an armored deck one inch deep to protect against plunging fire penetrating into the machinery spaces and magazines. Its maximum speed was 25 knots. The *Fearless* led the First Flotilla of destroyers while *Arethusa* led the Third Flotilla, comprising fifteen and sixteen ships respectively. These craft were among the newest destroyers of the Royal Navy.[6] Both of these flotillas comprised four divisions, with all but one of them, in the First Flotilla, possessing four vessels. Almost all of the ships in the First Flotilla were *Acheron*-class destroyers of the same class as Keyes's destroyer leaders. The Third Flotilla consisted of *Laforey*-class vessels. These ships possessed a marginally more powerful armament than the destroyers of the First Flotilla. The hull of a destroyer in this class measured 268' 10"×27' 8"×10' 6", was unarmored, and displaced between 965 tons and 1,010 tons. Such a ship mounted three 4-inch guns, one machine gun, and four 21-inch torpedo tubes. Its machinery produced a maximum speed of 29 knots.

At the same time as Tyrwhitt left Harwich, Rear Admiral Archibald Moore departed from his base at the Humber in command of the Second Battle Cruiser Squadron. This force, with orders to participate in the raid as supporting units, consisted of *Invincible* and *New Zealand*. Accompanying them was the Fourth Division of the First Flotilla of the Harwich Force, which comprised four destroyers. The battle cruiser *Invincible* was among the first of its type, being a vessel envisioned by former first sea lord Admiral John Fisher that incorporated the armament of a battleship with the hull and speed of a cruiser.[7] This ship, completed in March 1909, measured 567'×78' 6"×26' 2" and displaced 17,373 tons. It carried eight 12-inch guns in four dual-gunned turrets. One each was located in the bow and stern and the other two were placed on either side of the hull amidships. The ship also mounted sixteen 4-inch guns and five 18-inch torpedo tubes. The vessel's armor consisted primarily of a belt that varied between 6 inches and 4 inches in thickness and a protective deck up to 2.5 inches deep. The battle cruiser's engines yielded a maximum speed of 25.5 knots. These particulars were generally the same for the *New Zealand*, although the ship belonged to the *Indefatigable*-class and was completed over three years later. The key difference was that the *New Zealand* carried two fewer torpedo tubes.

The last of the British units originally designated for the raid into Heligoland Bight were those of the nominal commander of the Southern Force, Admiral Christian. This force steamed from Harwich on the night of 27 August, tasked with patrolling off Terschelling in search of German vessels that might be herded into the area by Tyrwhitt's forces. The five warships that regularly made up the squadron were armored cruisers of the *Bacchante*-class under the command of Rear Admiral H. H. Campbell. Christian, in overall command, flew his flag in *Euryalus*. These vessels, viewed with disdain by Keyes, could hardly be considered effective units for their mission. Completed between 1902 and 1904, all were already obsolete and ill-suited for the war in the North Sea. The hull of the *Euryalus* measured 472'×69' 6"×26' and displaced 12,000 tons.[8]

Armament consisted of two 9.2-inch guns, twelve 6-inch pieces, twelve 12-pound weapons, three 3-pound guns, and two 18-inch torpedo tubes. While the ship was well armed and had considerable armor, consisting primarily of a belt up to six inches thick and a protective deck of a maximum depth of three inches, its engines could produce a top speed of only 21 knots. This speed rendered it impossible for them to effectively pursue any of the German destroyers in the bight, as most of these possessed a maximum speed of 32 knots. The top speed of the German cruisers was somewhat less, but the slowest that entered combat in the Battle of Heligoland Bight had a maximum speed of 23 knots.

Unannounced to Keyes, Tyrwhitt, and Moore, and the source of a potential problem, were the additional forces dispatched by Jellicoe in the wake of his flurry of communiqués with the Admiralty. Before even informing the Admiralty of his decision, Jellicoe on the morning of 27 August dispatched the First Battle Cruiser Squadron of Vice Admiral David Beatty in support of the raid. Beatty got under way at 5:00 A.M. with his vessels, which like those of the majority of the force involved in the raid were among the newest of the fleet. The ships at Beatty's disposal also represented a concentration of some of the Grand Fleet's most powerful warships. Battle cruisers *Lion*, *Princess Royal*, and *Queen Mary* composed Beatty's squadron.[9] Beatty's flagship, *Lion*, and the *Princess Royal* were sister ships. Construction on both was complete in 1912. The hull of the *Lion* measured 700'×88' 6"×27' 8" and displaced 26,270 tons. An armor belt between 4 and 9 inches thick and an armored deck up to 2.5 inches deep served to protect it. The vessel carried eight 13.5-inch guns housed in four twin-gunned turrets. Two of these were located forward, and one each was cited amidships and aft. Augmenting this massive armament were sixteen 4-inch guns and two 21-inch torpedo tubes. The engines produced a maximum speed of 27 knots. The third vessel, *Queen Mary*, was in most respects a sister ship of the other two in Beatty's force, although the hull was slightly larger and its machinery produced a slightly higher maximum speed.

Jellicoe also dispatched the First Light Cruiser Squadron of Commodore William Goodenough with Beatty's battle cruisers. This force consisted of six *Town*-class light cruisers: *Southampton* (Goodenough's flagship), *Birmingham*, *Lowestoft*, *Nottingham*, *Falmouth*, and *Liverpool*. These ships made up three divisions of two warships each.[10] Although these warships represented three different classes of vessel, there was little difference in their technical specifications save for one. Goodenough's flagship, laid down in 1911 and completed the following year, was a vessel of the *Chatham*-class. The hull measured 458'× 49'×16', displaced 5,400 tons, and carried an armored belt and deck for protection. Armament consisted of eight 6-inch guns, four 3-pound weapons, and two 21-inch torpedo tubes. The engines produced 25.5 knots. The next three vessels in the list above, all vessels in the *Birmingham*-class, were completed in the same year as the outbreak of the war. The hull of one of these vessels measured

457'×50'×16', displaced 5,440 tons, and carried the same armor protection as *Southampton*. The only variation in armament from the flagship was an additional 6-inch gun. Its maximum speed was, like *Southampton's*, 25.5 knots. The *Falmouth* also had few differences from the *Southampton* and the other three, aside from being slightly smaller and slower, with a speed of 25 knots, and being protected only by a thin armored deck. The one ship of Goodenough's force that differed substantially from the others was the *Liverpool*, with an armament of two 6-inch guns, ten 4-inch weapons, four 3-pound guns, and two 18-inch torpedo tubes.

Confusion due to lack of information and coordination at the Admiralty surrounded the deployment of Beatty's and Goodenough's forces. Beatty, being the superior officer of both forces, proceeded to sea with scant information concerning the operation. As a result, he was able to signal at 8:00 A.M. to his vessels and those of Goodenough's only that "[w]e are to rendezvous with *Invincible* and *New Zealand* at . . . 5:00 a.m [on 28 August] to support destroyers and submarines . . . Operation consisting of a sweep . . . Heligoland to westward . . . Know very little, shall hope to learn more as we go along."[11] In keeping with the information he did have at his disposal, Beatty decided to join Rear Admiral Moore's two battle cruisers at a rendezvous position some ninety miles northwest of Heligoland. He accomplished this goal at 5:00 A.M. on 28 August.

Beatty's situation was far better than that of the main forces involved in the raid on Heligoland. While the situation produced by the scant information available to Beatty hampered his efforts to coordinate his forces with those of Tyrwhitt, Keyes, or Moore, the same problem threatened the operation as a whole. Although Admiral Christian, being the last of the original force to sortie, was made aware of the presence of Beatty and Goodenough, Tyrwhitt and Keyes steamed to Heligoland with no such information. The Admiralty attempted to warn them via wireless communication of the additional units taking part in the operation, but this message never reached them. Sometime around 1:00 P.M. on 27 August, the Admiralty dispatched a message to Harwich for transmission to Keyes and Tyrwhitt, but the wireless operators at the port shelved the message in lieu of their return. This action probably resulted from the fact that by this time the commanders were out of range for the receipt of a wireless transmission from Harwich.[12] Such an omission endangered all British ships at sea due to the possibility that British vessels might mistake one another for the enemy and engage. The danger was mostly posed to Beatty and Goodenough, because Tyrwhitt and Keyes had given instructions to their commanders that any large vessels other than the light cruisers of the Harwich Force should be considered hostile.

The potential for disaster first presented itself around 3:30 A.M. on 28 August as Tyrwhitt's force was about seventy miles north of Heligoland in the process of steaming for the starting position of the operation. Reports reached the commodore at this point that lookouts had sighted dark shapes approaching from astern. Tyrwhitt naturally assumed that they were enemy warships, but he had the foresight to issue a challenge by searchlight to the approaching craft. Surprise and relief ensued from the response that identified the unknown warships as those of Goodenough's light cruiser squadron. At this point, Tyrwhitt learned of all the additional supporting units when he signaled, "Are you taking part in the operation?" Goodenough replied, "Yes, I know your course and will support you. Beatty is behind us."[13] Tyrwhitt was surely pleased that the additional forces both he and Keyes had requested from the start were now a part of the operation, but he must also have quickly realized the problem for the raid overall. While he was now aware of the presence of more supporting units, Keyes with his submarines remained ignorant. The forces of Goodenough and Beatty would therefore potentially face the dangerous situation of mistaken identity that Tyrwhitt and Goodenough had barely avoided. Aside from the basic instruction that only Tyrwhitt's two light cruisers would be in the area of operations, Keyes had given his submarine commanders specific information to identify those cruisers. The *Arethusa* had one mast and three funnels, while *Fearless* had one mast and four funnels. The commodore had thereby instructed his commanders to treat any light cruiser with two masts and two, three, or four funnels as hostile because the Germans had no light cruisers matching the silhouette of Tyrwhitt's vessels.[14] All the vessels of Goodenough's force had two masts and four funnels, meaning that Keyes's commanders would treat them all as hostile and possibly destroy them. Beatty's battle cruisers also were in danger simply because the submarines were aware only of Moore's two battle cruisers, whose silhouettes were different from those of Beatty's battle cruisers. This situation presented a still greater threat to the British given the weather they encountered as they approached Heligoland Bight. While visibility had been good out to sea, a low-lying fog was present in the bight that reduced visibility from six thousand yards, or about 3.5 miles, to five thousand yards. Such conditions made ship identification more difficult than normal.

Amidst thickening fog and with these considerations in mind, Tyrwhitt and Goodenough steamed east-northeast toward the starting position of the operation. At 4:00 A.M. on 28 August, from a distance within sixty miles northwest of Heligoland, these forces turned south to begin the sweep into the bight. Tyrwhitt ordered his forces to make revolutions for 20 knots, although each ship kept up steam in their boilers for full speed. Goodenough's ships matched this action. Tyrwhitt in *Arethusa* led the sweep, with the Third Destroyer Flotilla cruising to port of his flagship. The ships of the flotilla maneuvered in line astern, with the four divisions separated by thousand-yard intervals. Captain Blunt in *Fearless*, with the First Destroyer Flotilla, steamed four thousand yards astern of Tyrwhitt's formation, with the destroyers disposed in the same manner. Commodore Goodenough's light cruisers were located sixteen thousand yards behind Blunt in three divisions. These three divisions of the First Light Cruiser Squadron cruised at intervals of four thousand yards from one another. Tyrwhitt intended to steam in this formation until he reached a point twelve miles west of Heligoland, when at around 8:00 A.M. he would alter course west to attack the forces of the German patrol in the rear.

As the British steamed closer to the area, lying in the fog were the units of the German Navy that they hoped to engage and destroy. While Vice Admiral Hipper had overall command of the defense, tactical command lay with his subordinate, Rear Admiral Leberecht Maas. This officer was both commander of the Second Scouting Group and senior officer of torpedo-boats. The force strength of the bight defense remained much as it was with the orders of 18 August that had reorganized the patrols. It consisted primarily of torpedo boats that varied in age and capability. The Germans by this time maintained their screen of patrolling torpedo boats at a distance of twenty-five miles from Heligoland. On the morning of 28 August, these were nine torpedo boats of Torpedo Boat Flotilla I, being the vessels V-187, which was the leader of the flotilla under Commander Wallis, V-188, V-189, V-190, V-191, G-193, G-194, G-196, and G-197. The first five of these vessels belonged to the same class, the V-180 type.[15] Such a ship measured 241' 6"×25' 9"×10' 3" and displaced 650 tons. Like most destroyers, the type had no armor. Its armament consisted of two 3.45-inch guns, one each placed in the bow and stern, and four 19.7-inch torpedo tubes. The vessel was capable of 32 knots. The other craft belonged to the G-192-class and were essentially identical. The design characteristics of these vessels are particularly significant for the Battle of Heligoland Bight. The Germans placed far more emphasis on their destroyers as torpedo attack vessels, which was the reason why they designated them torpedo boats. As a result, their gun armament was smaller in terms of both number and caliber than their British counterparts. As opposed to the Germans, the British placed emphasis on the ability of destroyers to sink vessels armed with torpedoes that might threaten the larger ships of the fleet. To this end, they had torpedoes, but more important were the guns. The larger number and size of guns in comparison to the Germans meant that the torpedo boats of the bight patrol were at a distinct disadvantage in terms of firepower and factored heavily into the damage sustained by these craft.

Twelve miles behind Torpedo Boat Flotilla I lay nine units of Minesweeping Division III under the charge of Lieutenant Commander Eberhard Wolfram. These craft represented a collection of older torpedo boats converted for minesweeping. As such, their combat potential was much less than that of their counterparts on the outer patrol. A typical example of these craft is D-8, which was Wolfram's vessel.[16] This ship was built in 1891, measured 196' 1"×24' 4"×11' 2", and displaced 404 tons. By the outbreak of war, its armament consisted of three 50mm guns and three 17.7-inch torpedo tubes. The vessel's maximum speed was only 22.5 knots, making it much slower than modern light craft. Others, such as

S-73, possessed the same limited capability. Built in the late nineteenth century, it mounted only one 50mm gun with its torpedo tubes.

In addition to these torpedo boats and minesweepers (which were merely older vessels of the former type) the patrol lines included supporting units. Among them were the light cruisers that escorted the patrols to and from their positions. On 28 August, four cruisers were on station in the area of Heligoland. Unfortunately for the Germans, these ships were among the weaker light cruisers of the patrolling forces and years older than the British light cruisers that raided into the bight, which hampered effective defense.[17] Closest to Heligoland, anchored to the north of the island, was the light cruiser *Stettin*, the most capable of the four. Built between 1906 and 1907, *Stettin* was commanded by Commander Karl August Nerger. This officer later captained the extremely successful commerce raider *Wolf*, which was an auxiliary cruiser, being a civilian vessel equipped with weapons. The hull of *Stettin* measured 383' 2"×43' 8"×17' 5" and displaced 3,480 tons. An armored deck varying between 1.75 inches and 0.75 inch thick protected the vessel's vital machinery and magazines from plunging shellfire. Its armament consisted of ten 4.1-inch guns, eight 2-inch pieces, and two 17.7-inch torpedo tubes. The ship's engines delivered a maximum speed of 23 knots. Two of the other vessels were units of a different class: the *Frauenlob* and the *Ariadne*, under the command of Captain Mommsen and Captain Seebohm respectively, were only slightly less capable than the *Stettin*. The former patrolled the region to the south of Heligoland, while the latter held a position farther south near the island of Wangerooge off the coast of Germany and near the mouth of the Jade River. Completed in 1903 and 1901 respectively, these vessels had hulls that measured 345' 1"×40' 1"×17' 9" and displaced 3,033 tons. Only an armored deck two inches thick protected the vessel amidships. The armament consisted of ten 4.1-inch guns and three 17.7-inch torpedo tubes. Like the *Stettin*, they possessed a maximum speed of 22 knots. The one vessel of almost no worth, the light cruiser *Hela*, patrolled an area farther north and east of the *Stettin*'s position. This vessel, completed in 1896, was totally obsolete. Its maximum speed was only 20 knots, and the ship's armament was barely equivalent to that of a British destroyer: four 3.45-inch guns, six 2-inch guns, and three 17.7-inch torpedo tubes. By comparison, the destroyers of Tyrwhitt's Third Flotilla carried three 4-inch guns and four 21-inch torpedo tubes.

Other light cruisers lay at points around the Heligoland Bight defense for further support of the patrols, although they would have to raise steam to participate in battle.[18] One of these was the *Köln*, the flagship of Rear Admiral Maas, which retired from Heligoland during the night of 27 August, bound for Wilhelmshaven to coal. The light cruiser *Mainz*, a sister ship of the *Köln*, under the command of Captain Wilhelm Pasche, lay at the mouth of the Ems River. Another six light cruisers were anchored in either Wilhelmshaven or Brunsbüttel. In the former port were *Strassburg*, *Stralsund*, and *Rostock*, while *Kolberg* lay in

Schillig Roads just off Wilhelmshaven. The light cruisers *Danzig* and *München*, after having been detached for duty in the Baltic Sea, were anchored by 28 August at the latter port.

These light cruisers possessed similar design characteristics despite their being units of multiple classes. Completed between 1909 and 1910, the light cruisers *Köln*, *Mainz*, and *Kolberg* belonged to one class. The hull of the *Köln* measured 426' 6"×46'×17' 7" and displaced 4,362 tons. Protection consisted of an armored deck, while the armament comprised twelve 4.1-inch guns, two 17.7-inch torpedo tubes, and one hundred mines. The maximum speed of the ship was 26.7 knots. The light cruisers *Strassburg* and *Stralsund* belonged to another class completed in early 1914, but were generally similar in their specifications, the difference being larger torpedo tubes and the addition of an armor belt for protection. The *Rostock* was a faster version of *Strassburg* and *Stralsund*. Less capable than all of these were *Ariadne*, *Danzig*, and *München* that were all slightly older. While *Aridane* was completed in 1901 as a unit of one class and the other two were completed in 1907 and 1905 respectively as part of another class, they all had an armament that consisted of ten 4.1-inch guns and two 17.7-inch torpedo tubes. Their maximum speeds varied between 21.5 and 23 knots. All of these supporting light cruisers shared a similarity with those on patrol at Heligoland. Like the destroyers of the bight defense, these cruisers carried smaller guns than their British counterparts. Consequently, in terms of ship-to-ship comparison of combat ability, they were outmatched.

The defense of the bight comprised two more elements on the opening of battle, one that was directly attached to the effort and another that could potentially support if needed. The former consisted of more naval units, including the ten vessels of Torpedo Boat Flotilla V, with characteristics similar to those of Torpedo Boat Flotilla I. On 28 August, these ships were anchored in the artificial harbor built at the southern end of Heligoland. Although they were normally kept in bases on Germany's North Sea coast, the German naval command decided to relocate them. This decision came after, at 6:00 P.M. on 27 August, aircraft reconnaissance spotted an enemy destroyer fifty miles west of Texel, Netherlands, steaming southwest.[19] The other group were capital ships of the German High Seas Fleet that lay at Wilhelmshaven. Hipper's battle cruisers—the *Seydlitz*, the vice admiral's flagship, *Moltke*, and the *Von Der Tann*—formed part of this group.. These three vessels counted as some of the most powerful in the fleet. The flagship and the *Moltke*, although being units of two different classes, shared virtually the same characteristics.[20] The hull of *Seydlitz* measured 657' 11"×93' 6"×26' 11", displaced 24,594 tons, and relied on armor protection that consisted in part of a belt with a maximum thickness of twelve inches. The vessel mounted ten 11.1-inch guns in five dual-piece turrets, twelve 5.9-inch guns, twelve 3.45-inch weapons, and four 19.7-inch torpedo tubes. The ship's engines produced a maximum speed of 26.5 knots. Only nominally weaker was *Von Der Tann*, which was slightly slower and possessed a different armament, being in part eight 11.1-inch guns. In addition to these ships, Hipper also had charge of the armored cruiser *Blucher*, although on 28 August it was coaling at Wilhelmshaven. These ships, however, could not directly support the forces in the bight unless the tide allowed them to cross the Jade Bar. The high command did not consider this problematic as naval officials assumed that the British would employ only light forces, such as cruisers, submarines, and destroyers, in a raid on the bight. The decision to locate them behind the Jade Bar, however, served to cripple the defense of the bight in the event that the British did indeed employ heavy warships. The German official history of the war justly characterized the high command's assumption as "a fatal error."[21]

The second element was the island of Heligoland itself. Although small, Heligoland became a formidable fortress in the expanse of the North Sea. On 1 August 1914, German Vice Admiral von Krosigk, the chief of the headquarters of the North Sea Naval Stations, had forcefully removed the two thousand inhabitants of the island in order to transform it strictly into a naval installation. By the time Krosigk expelled the islanders, the process of fortification was already essentially complete. As Germany had already possessed the island since 1890, the process unfolded quickly: within a week of the transfer, construction began on a barracks, a light railway, and a fortified battery. The latter endeavor formed part of the armament. By 28 August, it consisted of four 4.1-inch guns, these being placed at points on the artificial harbor at the southern tip of the island, and two 3.5-inch guns on the northern end of Heligoland.[22] The island fortress also boasted a Zeppelin shed for the purpose of reconnaissance. All the installations of Heligoland, particularly the guns and the southern harbor, benefited from steps taken to guard against the possibility of massive erosion of the island's two-hundred-foot-high cliffs by the elements. Central to these was the effort to reinforce the shores of the island with concrete and granite.

At 6:30 A.M. on 28 August, the British were nearing a position to test the value of the defenses placed at Heligoland as well as those of the German patrols. Tyrwhitt approached the outer patrol line in the same formation he had assumed at the start of the cruise toward Heligoland. Most of Keyes's submarines were in position, with the commodore and his destroyers being with the outer line of decoy craft. Beatty and Moore's forces lay some forty miles to the north of Tyrwhitt.

The Germans by this time already had a hint that something was afoot in the bight. Shortly after 6:00 A.M., torpedo boat *G-194*, captained by Lieutenant Commander Buss, lay in its sector of the outer patrol in a position northwest of Heligoland. Although the sky was overcast and the dreary weather included heavy fog that hampered visibility, the surface of the sea was calm. This led to the relatively easy sighting of two periscopes about fifty-five yards to starboard. These denoted the presence of *E-9*, which had orders to serve as part of the inner line of submarines near Heligoland. Its periscopes, however, disappeared seconds after their sighting, as lookouts also spotted a heavy swirl in the water that denoted the discharge of torpedoes. According to the Germans, the wakes of two of these underwater weapons passed underneath the ship, owing largely to the shallow draft of its hull. In actuality, the British submarine only fired one torpedo. Nevertheless, Buss ordered an attack on the British ship. This effort failed, however, as the submarine dove deep before Buss could arrive at its position. Destroyers in 1914 did not have depth charges, as technological development had not yet produced viable weapons of this type. Consequently, destroyers in early World War I could sink only a submarine that lay just beneath the surface of the water, by ramming it. Despite the abortive attack, Buss used his wireless to send a message to Rear Admiral Maas aboard the *Köln:* "Was attacked 6 A.M. by a submerged submarine in center square 142 epsilon [denoting on a map of the bight where the engagement took place], two torpedoes, not hit. Saw the periscope distance 50 m. False alarm impossible. Enemy submarine steering NW."[23]

Maas did not react to the message immediately because of a mistake made by the wireless operator of the *Köln* when he decoded the message. At first, the time of Buss's report read 2:25 A.M. rather than the real time, 6:05 A.M., which prompted Maas to radio back to Buss for clarification. The torpedo boat commander then retransmitted the report. Further delay resulted when Maas forwarded the report to Hipper. This time lag, although it resulted in a delayed response to events in the bight that hampered its defense for the entire day, was not entirely a product of poor communication on the part of the Germans. Rather, it was a common element in early wireless communication. The Germans transmitted most messages in code, which was necessary because any vessel, whether friend or enemy, could hear the signal if their wireless sets were tuned to the same frequency. The process of receiving and decoding the message normally meant that the command of a vessel did not receive the communiqué until ten to fifteen minutes after it was sent. Further time elapsed when the commander composed a response and his wireless officers encoded and transmitted the appropriate orders. As a result, only at 7:12 A.M. did Hipper act. Based on Buss's report, he concluded that the bight was being attacked solely by submarines and issued commands accordingly. The vice admiral radioed to Heligoland at 7:10 A.M. that Torpedo Boat Flotilla V put to sea to search for enemy submarines. He transmitted the same directive to Maas. Hipper also sent out aircraft for reconnaissance, being "aircraft 59," but the low-lying fog in the bight that morning made the mission impossible.

While these measures unfolded, at 6:53 A.M. Tyrwhitt's surface units made their first contact with the units of the German outer patrol in a position some twenty-four miles northwest of Heligoland. At this time, in weather conditions where fog limited visibility to five thousand yards, the units of the Fourth Division of Tyrwhitt's Third Destroyer Flotilla—*Laurel, Liberty, Lysander,* and *Laertes*—sighted smoke off their port side at a distance of three miles. This destroyer once again proved to be G-194 under Buss. Tyrwhitt ordered the flotilla, which was nearest to the unknown craft, to chase it through the thickening fog while the rest of the force continued the sweep. Within five minutes, one of the destroyers issued a light signal challenge for the identity of the craft. By this time, Buss had reversed his course in order to make full speed toward the defenses of Heligoland and Torpedo Boat Flotilla V. While he was making the dash for safety, the destroyer *Laurel* opened the surface action with fire that landed some eight hundred yards short of Buss's vessel. Simultaneously, Buss was radioing the presence of British surface vessels in the bight. The message, sent to the *Köln*, stated that Buss believed himself under attack by enemy cruisers and gave their position. British wireless operators, however, managed to jam the transmission of this message. Only the other vessels of the patrol adjacent in their positions to G-194 had the possibility of receiving the message. These were G-196 to the northeast and V-187 to the southwest. The former vessel, at a distance of some 7.5 miles from G-194 at the time, steered toward the sound of the gunfire through the fog. The vessel's commander also relayed Buss's message to the *Köln* at 7:06 A.M. The latter craft, which was the flagship of Torpedo Boat Flotilla I under the command of Lieutenant Commander Lechler and also shipped the commander of the flotilla, Commander Wallis, also steered to the sound of the guns. At 7:20 A.M., Lechler was able to report to Maas the presence of two enemy destroyers, although V-187 did not ultimately join the battle.[24] Lechler later established that the vessels he had seen were cruisers and accordingly altered his course east-southeast toward Heligoland alone.

While Lechler pursued this course of action, some fourteen minutes after the engagement started G-196 arrived to aid Buss. Together G-194 and G-196 quickly shaped a course south-southeast and continued the running firefight in which G-194 had already been engaged. Contrary to the assertions of some books that detail the Battle of Heligoland Bight, the German dash for Heligoland was not done in keeping with a standing plan to lure attacking vessels closer to the guns of Heligoland and the light cruisers that awaited there. Rather, this action was the only one open to these vessels as both fled a stronger enemy force and steered for a source of support.[25] In the ensuing action, fog and the resulting low visibility hampered the fire of ships on both sides. Indeed, the aft gun crew of G-196 got off only fourteen shots.[26] The Germans could only bring their stern guns to bear as they raced to Heligoland, which was a wise policy since by this time it was clear to the torpedo boat captains that they faced a superior British force. Buss could now identify at least nine British destroyers and two cruisers. At 7:26 A.M., Tyrwhitt, who had lost sight of the Fourth Division of Third Flotilla, altered course due east toward them. The Germans as a result faced far more elements of the Harwich Force than they had initially.

The correctness of Tyrwhitt's decision made itself felt when his lookouts soon reported the sighting of ten destroyers. These were other vessels of Torpedo Boat Flotilla I as well as those of Torpedo Boat Flotilla V. The commanders of these ships were totally unprepared for the encounter with British surface units. The lead boat in the formation of the latter group of torpedo boats, G-9 under the command of Lieutenant Commander Anschutz, was the only one to appreciate the situation, due solely to the advantage that the craft had in terms of its position in relation to the others. Even after sighting the British destroyers and seeing the flash of gunfire, Anschutz believed that the vessels he saw ahead could be friendly. Only after noting the position of their smokestacks and bridge structures did he conclude that they were hostile and opened fire. Probably due in part to the rapidly unfolding events and the drawbacks in German communication, Maas had not updated Anschutz and the commanders of the other vessels about the presence of British warships other than the submarines that they had first been ordered to pursue. Maas's reaction was quite slow as he had first received an inkling that there might be British surface forces through the report from G-196 at 7:06 A.M. about the presence of enemy cruisers. Maas's slow reaction accounts for the belated message he received at 7:29 A.M. from Torpedo Boat Flotilla V that they were under fire.[27]

The situation as a result was one of mass confusion and great peril for the German torpedo boats. All elements of the British Third Destroyer Flotilla were entering battle along with Tyrwhitt in *Arethusa*, who altered his course at 7:40 A.M. to east-southeast. To the northwest of the commodore at a distance of about four miles was Captain Blunt in *Fearless*, along with the First Destroyer Flotilla. The distance kept these craft from opening fire on the Germans. Those German vessels of Torpedo Boat Flotilla V behind G-9 at first did not appreciate their situation, believing that G-9 was in action with a submarine. Aboard torpedo boat V-2, lookouts sighted shell splashes around G-9 that they assumed were from a British submarine's deck gun. Another vessel of the flotilla, being V-1, mistook the same splashes for a torpedo. When all realized the situation as British destroyers appeared through the mist, they reversed course for Heligoland with the British close behind in a running firefight similar to that between the British Fourth Division of the Third Flotilla and G-194 and G-196. Those vessels of Torpedo Boat Flotilla I, the original outer patrol in the bight, managed to largely avoid being caught in this stage of the sweep, although V-188 reported being fired on by a British submarine

The vessels of Torpedo Boat Flotilla I were quite fortunate compared to those of the other flotilla. Before their reversal of course was even complete, the vessels of Torpedo Boat Flotilla V came under British fire. The situation quickly became dire for the hard-pressed craft. Some craft of the flotilla first sought to engage the British before the force composition of the enemy was completely known. Chief among these was V-6 under Lieutenant Commander Hooffert, who closed to within 3,250 yards and opened fire. Only minutes later did Anschutz issue the general order to steam for Heligoland. Upon this signal, the ships of the force formed a line abreast where a distance of some 650 yards separated each craft. All maintained fire at the British with their aft guns, although accuracy was rather poor owing to the fog as well as smoke produced from the destroyers themselves. In a fighting retreat, the smoke produced by their fires wafted aft over the guns in action and obscured the sea beyond. German shot in this stage of the action, according to a German reconnaissance plane, generally fell short of the pursuing British largely because of the smaller caliber of the German guns as opposed to the British. Fire also was erratic owing to poor visibility from weather conditions. The latter problem resulted in few rounds actually being fired—between fifteen and thirty shots for most of the craft in the flotilla.[28] The only comfort taken from this poor performance was the fact that, in part again from the fog, the British fire was also ineffective.

This poor situation for the Germans unfolded as the range between the opposing ships closed steadily. As the distance decreased, the possibility of being destroyed by the numerically superior British forces increased greatly. The vessels of Torpedo Boat Flotilla V were not able to outdistance their pursuers or even maintain the interval between them. This had nothing to do with any technical difference in speed, as their design capabilities in terms of speed were similar to the British. The problem lay with the condition of their engines. The rigors of constant patrol duty wore heavily on the engines of these craft, and many of them were unable to raise steam for full power and sustain it for a prolonged chase. At highest risk were torpedo boats V-1 and S-13. The latter, under the command of Lieutenant Commander Adolf Müller, suffered engine problems that reduced its speed to 20 knots. Still worse were the problems of V-1, under the command of Lieutenant Commander Siess, which by 7:50 A.M. placed the vessel within four thousand yards of the British.

These vessels bore the brunt of British fire, and their survival was in the balance. Siess's vessel was the first to suffer, as shell splashes blanketed the torpedo boat. At 7:50 A.M., the shell from a 4-inch gun hit the upper deck amidships and penetrated the aft stoke hold, the compartment that housed boilers and furnaces. This hit killed one of the crew and wounded two others and also forced the evacuation of the compartment. The damage and the consequent abandoning of the area slowed the ship to 20 knots, making its position still worse in the face of the approaching British. Soon afterward, a second hit landed in the starboard coal bunker underneath the bridge, although the coal in this compartment largely absorbed the blast and consequently decreased the shell's damaging effect. Even so, the hit was serious for V-1, as it caused damage to one of the ship's turbines and rudder control from the hail of splinters resulting from the explosion. The ordeal of V-1, as well as the generally unfavorable situation overall, prompted Anschutz to radio to Maas at 7:45 A.M. that cruiser aid was requested. By the time this letter was issued, Hipper had already issued orders to that effect.[29]

The call for cruisers was particularly necessary given that by this time additional German vessels were under fire from the British. As Tyrwhitt's forces proceeded toward Heligoland, some of the destroyers passed through Torpedo Boat Flotilla V in the mist and came upon elements of Minesweeping Division III that formed the inner patrol line in the bight. At 7:30 A.M., the minesweepers, all obsolete torpedo boats, under the command of Lieutenant Commander Eberhard Wolfram, sighted units of Torpedo Boat Flotilla V emerging from the mist, and moments later Tyrwhitt's *Arethusa* and Third Flotilla in pursuit. This encounter came as a complete surprise to every craft of the force since only one craft was fitted with a wireless set.[30]Another reason for the lack of preparation was the fact that the division leader, *D-8* under the command of Lieutenant Commander Wolfram, did not have sufficient information despite his vessel being equipped with the only wireless set in the division. At 7:15 A.M., Wolfram and his crew had observed the sound of gunfire, but believed that it was gunnery practice.[31] The only wireless message that Wolfram received was the first of the day from *G-196* that signaled the presence of only submarines. Thus, Wolfram patrolled his region in search of the reported craft. The lieutenant commander was also unaware simply because of the communication lag between Maas, Hipper, and the forces in the bight. Wolfram did the best he could in the circumstances: "As soon as the hostile craft could be seen more clearly— one cruiser and 10 to 14 destroyers [being *Arethusa* and the Third Flotilla] were made out—I opened fire with the port bridge gun and stern gun. As the range was decreasing, I turned to starboard to show the stern to the enemy."[32] Wolfram, as well as the other vessels of his force, shaped a course in keeping with the other German warships already in flight. They had little choice, as their outmoded armament could not hope to match that of the British vessels.

This maneuver did Wolfram's command little good, owing to the difference in speed between his ships and those of the British. The lieutenant commander's flagship could muster only 22.5 knots against the 29 knots of the units in the British Third Flotilla. Even *Arethusa* could best the speed of Wolfram with 25 knots. Part of Wolfram's force avoided this situation as they were not sighted by the British. Those ships of the force that the British spotted, however—*D-8*, *S-73*, *T-34*, *T-33*, and *T-37*—were in danger of being overrun and destroyed. The range between the British and some of these ships closed steadily to between four thousand and one thousand yards.

Wolfram's ship suffered most, with five hits. This number could have been far higher, but British accuracy was still not great. During the forty minutes that he was under fire, Wolfram himself counted six hundred shell splashes in the region of his craft, while observers on Heligoland, who could now just see the action as it approached them, counted two hundred in the last portion of the firefight. In response, the crew of the aft gun in *D-8* fired eighty-five shells from their 2-inch gun. The diminutive size of this weapon meant that the shells caused no damage. While the number of British shells fired seems a bit high, it is clear that *D-8* proved exceedingly fortunate. The minesweeper was certainly in danger of being sunk. One larger shell, from the *Arethusa*, penetrated the side of the hull to the engine room, but apparently did not explode. It only dented the bulkhead to the engine compartment. A second hit also did little damage. The third, however, shredded the side of the ship both above and below the waterline, while a fourth hit the bridge. The explosion from the impact of this shell, which was apparently high explosive ordnance, started a large fire, killed the captain of the ship, Lieutenant Weiffenbach, and wounded sixteen to twenty men. This hit broke steam lines that fed the engines, which decreased the vessel's already low speed. By the end of the battle, Wolfram's ship suffered eleven men dead and nineteen wounded.

The possibility of *S-73*, *T-34*, *T-33*, and *T-37* escaping the ordeal being undergone by Wolfram seemed slight. The first of these, although escaping unscathed, came under fire for seven minutes. Minesweepers *T-34* and *T-37* managed to escape, but *T-33* was not so lucky. This ship wildly zigzagged to try to throw off the rangefinders aboard the British ships. With the range down to two thousand yards, Lieutenant Commander Kaehlert also opened fire at *Arethusa* with his aft gun. This spirited action, however, did not ward off the two hits that caused flooding in the engine room that forced its evacuation. The ship glided to a halt, dead in the water and at the mercy of the approaching British.

The situation of both Wolfram's ships and those of Torpedo Boat Flotilla V proved dire, but ultimately the British did not sink any of the craft in either force. Minesweepers *D-8* and *T-33*, which were later towed to safety, and all of the other vessels owed their survival to the appearance at 7:57 A.M. of German light cruisers in the area. This forced the British to redirect their fire toward the more powerful units of the enemy.

These vessels proved to be the light cruisers *Stettin* and *Frauenlob*, which were both a part of the supporting cruiser forces for the Heligoland defense. The former ship, being the most capable of the Heligoland force under the command of Captain Karl Nerger, first appeared through the mists to the lookouts on board Tyrwhitt's flagship. Up until 7:36 A.M., light cruiser *Stettin* remained anchored at its position just northeast of Heligoland. At the time, Nerger received reports on the positions of enemy vessels in the bight. These reports placed Nerger in an unfavorable position. He appreciated the need for his vessel to engage the enemy as quickly as possible, but *Stettin* was not completely battle ready. Only eight of the ship's eleven boilers were producing steam to power the systems of the ship, meaning that it was not capable of its maximum speed should it be needed in combat. Nevertheless, Nerger exhibited the leadership qualities that led to his later success in command of the German commerce raider *Wolf* when he gave orders to proceed at all possible speed—a maximum of only 15 knots at the time—toward the position noted in the reports and the sound of gunfire. Reception of the 7:45 A.M. call for the aid of cruisers from Torpedo Boat Flotilla V merely confirmed the correctness of his decision. This action occurred through Nerger's own initiative. The captain weighed anchor before receiving at 7:47 A.M. the order from Hipper to "hunt enemy destroyers."[33] The wording of this order indicates that Hipper still believed that his forces faced primarily a collection of destroyers; in keeping with the basic assumption of the high command, he certainly did not believe that the battle cruisers of Beatty were in the bight. In terms of naval units around Heligoland, it should be noted that at the same time Nerger received the message to "hunt destroyers," so too did Captain Otto Feldman, in command of the Second U-Boat Flotilla. Of the six submarines anchored in the artificial harbor of Heligoland, only two, *U-16* and *U-25*, were able to respond immediately. At 8:09 A.M., these vessels cleared Heligoland to take up positions north and south of the island. They played no significant part in the battle.[34] The same message sent to the *Stettin* reached Captain Mommsen in the *Frauenlob* three minutes later. He too raised steam and proceeded on a course due north from his position south of Heligoland.

Upon sighting the *Stettin* off his port bow to the northeast, Tyrwhitt altered his course slightly farther east as he made preparations to engage. At the same time, however, lookouts sighted the *Frauenlob* off the port bow, as by this time the German light cruiser had made all possible speed to a position just south of the *Stettin*. Tyrwhitt decided to engage the *Frauenlob* and leave the *Stettin* to Captain Blunt in the light cruiser *Fearless* along with the destroyers of First Flotilla, which had until this point been too distant from the battle to take part. Tyrwhitt consequently altered course south-southwest, as did the *Frauenlob*, as the destroyers of Third Flotilla broke off their pursuit in light of the arrival of the German light cruisers and made back for Tyrwhitt's flagship.

By the time of Tyrwhitt's decision, Captain Nerger had already issued the order to engage the British. At first, Nerger opened fire on Tyrwhitt's force at a range of some 9,300 yards. This fire was ineffective, as were a few rounds loosed by ships of Tyrwhitt's command before the commodore turned to face the *Frauenlob*. At the time that Tyrwhitt disengaged from the *Stettin*, the German vessel had halted its fire. A report that the British vessels were actually German torpedo boats gave Nerger pause. By the time that the error was cleared up, the German captain saw that Tyrwhitt's ships were out of range, having already pursued their new course.

The respite in the engagement, however, lasted only a few short minutes; at 8:05 A.M. Blunt in the *Fearless* as well as some destroyers in the First Flotilla engaged Nerger's ship. The capable gun crews of the British vessels, particularly the *Fearless*, quickly achieved straddling shots so numerous that witnesses on board craft in the fleeing Torpedo Boat Flotilla V likened it to the *Stettin's* being in boiling water. Indeed, so many shells landed in proximity to the German light cruiser that Nerger could not discern whether or not the fire was coming from Blunt's vessel: "Whether this cruiser took part in the battle is not definitely established. The impacts of hostile shells were so numerous in the immediate vicinity of the ship that this could not be observed."[35] Even so, over the entire engagement that lasted only five minutes at ranges between 9,300 yards and 5,050 yards, the *Stettin* only suffered one hit. This came from the *Fearless* at a range of 8,000 yards and knocked the vessel's Number 4 gun on the starboard side out of action. The blast killed two of the gun crew and wounded another. At this point, Nerger made the decision to retire to Sellebrunnen Buoy. Although his ship was not seriously damaged, Nerger was aware by 8:10 A.M. that the units of Torpedo Boat Flotilla V were safe under the protection of the guns on Heligoland island. The captain had thus accomplished his mission in part, and the torpedo boats did not take part in subsequent operations. While the units of Minesweeping Division III still remained in danger, Nerger believed that he needed to retire at this point in order to raise steam in all of his ship's boilers and thus give him the full power that the ship needed for combat. Captain Blunt accommodated him when he too broke off the engagement to resume the sweep with Tyrwhitt.

As a result of the *Stettin's* action, only the units of Torpedo Boat Flotilla I and Minesweeping Division III remained at sea in the face of the British. Five units of the former were en route to the Jade River, while a sixth, flotilla leader *V-187*, was on a course toward Heligoland. These ships steamed undetected, but the minesweepers remained in serious trouble through the harassing fire of the British. A further light cruiser engagement, however, allowed the minesweepers to safely disengage.

This action began at 8:10 A.M., as the engagement between the *Stettin* and the *Fearless* came to an end, when the *Frauenlob* and the *Arethusa* commenced firing on one another at an opening range of 6,000 yards. The encounter, lasting only fifteen minutes, was one that pitted against one another vessels that were fairly evenly matched in terms of their capabilities. Mommsen's ship counted ten 4.1-inch guns in its armament, while *Arethusa* shipped two 6-inch guns and six 4-inch weapons. The 6-inch guns of the British ship gave an advantage in range over the German vessel, but this was negated as the range closed steadily during the action until reaching about 3,500 yards. Tyrwhitt also possessed an advantage of 3 knots in speed over his German opponent, but this difference was negligible. Even so, in this engagement Tyrwhitt was at a slight disadvantage given the condition of his vessel. The same problem with the ejectors of the 4-inch guns that had forced an end to gunnery practice on 27 August now lessened the combat effectiveness of the ship. Two of *Arethusa's* guns jammed at the opening of the battle and thus reduced the ship's weight of fire against the German vessel. In addition, the *Arethusa's* performance suffered from the crew's inexperience with their new ship. Mommsen's vessel, on the other hand, benefited from a seasoned crew.

The experience of the German crew made itself felt quickly as the third salvo from the *Frauenlob* resulted in shell splashes that straddled Tyrwhitt's flagship. This signaled that the German vessel had the range. Over the next few minutes, the Germans scored fifteen direct hits on the port side of the British vessel through very accurate fire, the first landing abreast Number 3 funnel with the fourth salvo. Mommsen's ship might have landed as many as thirty-five hits on Tyrwhitt's flagship. These hits caused a great deal of damage to *Arethusa* that told heavily on the ship's combat capability. By 8:25 A.M., only one 6-inch gun remained in action, while all of the 4-inch guns were disabled from either having jammed or being damaged by enemy shellfire. In terms of enemy gunfire, one that hit just aft of the fourth funnel ignited the cordite charges that fed Number 2 port gun. According to eyewitnesses aboard minesweeper *T-33*, which was in sight of the battle, a large yellowish-red sheet of flame, indicative of a cordite fire, erupted from this area of the ship. Chief Petty Officer Frederick Wrench promptly put out the blaze on deck, but the gun was out of action.[36] All of the torpedo tubes were also out of action. In addition to losing offensive capability, the ship also lost propulsion. One of the German shells exploded in the *Arethusa's* main feed tank. In naval vessels, this device holds water that is pumped through the propulsion system to create the steam that drives the engines. Damage to this vital piece of machinery steadily decreased the *Arethusa's* speed. In addition, shrapnel from some of the *Stettin's* shells knocked out the wireless as well as all of the ship's searchlights. So heavy was the shrapnel damage that it led one British officer to comment that "her [*Arethusa's*] decks and bridge were completely serrated and peppered with holes and marks, which left her a sorry sight."[37] Another good indication of the amount of shrapnel that swept the *Arethusa* came from events after the action. Crewmembers claimed that in several parts of the ship one could pick up handfuls of shrapnel pieces.[38] Despite the damage, however, the *Arethusa* suffered few casualties: eleven killed and sixteen wounded. Among the dead was Signal Officer Lieutenant Eric Westmacott. The circumstances that caused his demise could have killed Tyrwhitt himself; Westmacott, who stood next to Tyrwhitt on the bridge, was in the process of pointing out the cordite fire when shrapnel struck the young officer down. All told, Tyrwhitt was certainly impressed by the Germans' accuracy and by the situation overall, as he later wrote to his wife that "I was so surprised that so many projectiles could fall all round one and burst in all directions and yet so few people killed. . . . We had fifteen direct hits on the side and waterline and many in board, besides hundreds of shrapnel holes."[39] A further letter to his sister described the scene a bit more vividly. Tyrwhitt wrote that "[t]he air seemed thick with bursting shells and the sea was alive with splashes and shell splinters."[40]

The destroyers of Tyrwhitt's force could have aided their flagship, but events deprived the commodore of many of them. Chief among these was a case of mistaken identity resulting from the fog, when British destroyers engaged what they believed was a German minelayer. In truth, the ship proved to be the 731-ton Norwegian steamer *Kong Guttorm* under the command of Captain Laurithson that normally ran between Christiania (now Oslo), Norway, and Bremen, Germany. Upon the outbreak of battle, Laurithson was on a course toward Heligoland to pick up a German pilot for the leg of the voyage into Bremen. His ship simply suffered the misfortune of being in the wrong place at the wrong time. British fire ceased only when the Norwegian vessel established its neutrality to the satisfaction of the attacking destroyers through hoisting the Norwegian flag. By this time, the craft had suffered three injured due to splinters produced by numerous, though nonfatal, hits.[41] Other British destroyers remained engaged with *T-33* until the close of the contest between the light cruisers. A few of the destroyers launched a torpedo attack against the German light cruiser, but these proved unsuccessful.

The lack of much destroyer support and the damage to the *Arethusa*, however, did not allow the *Frauenlob* to escape unscathed, although its damage proved far lighter than that inflicted on its opponent. Soon after Mommsen opened fire on the *Arethusa*, he observed shell splashes close to his vessel. His ship subsequently suffered ten hits. The forward 6-inch gun of the *Arethusa* scored most of these. One shell hit the port side of the conning tower from which Mommsen controlled his ship. Another landed in the crow's nest of the forward mast. The destruction of the mast knocked out the *Frauenlob's* wireless communication because the ship's radio yards were strung from it. An additional 6-inch hit penetrated the hull and holed the warship's protective deck, while several others penetrated at points along the side of the hull. None of these produced any flooding because they all created holes above the waterline. In all, the *Frauenlob* suffered five dead and thirty-two wounded from these hits. All of these were crewmen in the exposed areas of the ship: gun crews, range-finder crews, ammunition passers, and lookouts in the crow's nest. This suggests the extent of the damage to the German ship. Aside from the damage to its wireless, the ship's fighting capability was not impaired.

Nevertheless, Mommesen at 8:25 A.M. decided to break off the engagement and shaped a course to the east. Several accounts of the battle record that the German captain's decision was the result of the hit to the *Frauenlob's* bridge, which it is claimed badly damaged the bridge of the ship and forced its retirement. This assertion appears to stem from the after-action report of Tyrwhitt to the Admiralty concerning the battle. The commodore wrote that "a 6-inch projectile from the *Arethusa* wrecked the fore bridge of the enemy, who had once turned away in the direction of Heligoland."[42] Actually, the sight of the explosion proved far more spectacular than the damage caused by the shell. Indeed, the same can be said about many of the hits registered on Mommsen's vessel, owing to an apparent defect in British shells. Several members of the ship's crew observed British shells that did not explode upon hitting the water, while one shell that hit the *Frauenlob* penetrated an airshaft and fell into the vessel's broadside torpedo room. Had it detonated, the explosion probably would have set off the torpedoes and led to the destruction of the ship. Instead, crewmembers subsequently discovered it intact after the battle. Some members of the *Kong Guttorm's* crew had the same experience. They later claimed to have found an unexploded shell in the ship's cargo hold.[43] One can only conjecture what the fate of the *Frauenlob* and other vessels of the German defense might have been without this problem with British ordnance. It certainly hampered the effectiveness of the British attack and thereby diminished the overall success of the raid.

Rather than breaking off the engagement as a result of damage, Mommsen decided to do so because he learned, like Nerger on the *Stettin*, that his primary mission of saving the torpedo boats had been achieved. British actions facilitated the retreat, as around the same time Mommsen altered course, Tyrwhitt's forces broke off their engagement. This also saved the vessels of Minesweeping Division III. Mommsen was free to tow *T-33* out of the combat area en route to Heligoland before making a course for Wilhelmshaven.

Tyrwhitt disengaged as the result of four factors. One was certainly the damage to his flagship, but more important was the perceived danger to the entire force stemming from the proximity to Heligoland. At the time that the engagement ended, the mists on the surface of the ocean cleared enough to reveal Heligoland only five miles distant. By the time that the *Frauenlob* retired, however, the guns of Heligoland were not actually a threat to the British despite the proximity of the sides. The Germans had cleared their guns for battle beginning at 7:30 A.M. when gunfire was heard through the fog. While they completed preparations at 7:50 A.M. and saw destroyers passing the island a few minutes later, the Germans could not identify them as friend or foe. Even had they been able to identify the craft, the fog also prevented accurate calculation of range to the targets. Consequently, Heligoland played no role in the battle. Even so, the British, not knowing how hampered Heligoland's defenders were by the fog, wished to get out of the range of the guns on the island. In addition, Tyrwhitt believed that most of the torpedo boats and minesweepers, being the object of the raid to this point, had escaped. Finally, the commodore was concerned that his forces were too dispersed. Consequently, the commodore ordered a change of course due west away from the island at a speed of 20 knots. The Harwich Force steered to a course west-southwest with the Third Flotilla cruising in line ahead near the *Arethusa* and the First Flotilla in line abreast of the *Fearless*.

Upon the turn to the west, the battle had certainly not led to the success envisioned by both Keyes and Tyrwhitt during the planning stage of the operation. No German vessels were sunk, although at the time the British believed they had sunk minesweeper *T-33*, and while Tyrwhitt turned away from Heligoland, most of the vessels still at sea that had been the intended prey of the raid escaped. This collection of craft comprised the last of the minesweepers at sea and also four torpedo boats of the First Torpedo Boat Flotilla. The latter were *V-189*, *V-190*, *V-191*, and *G-197*, which all patrolled the southern portion of the outer patrol line. These vessels first tried to cruise to Heligoland, but at 8:25 A.M., upon sighting the *Arethusa* and the Third Flotilla steering toward them, the warships briefly engaged the British before retiring east-southeast toward the Jade River. The unsatisfactory nature of the raid was exacerbated by the damage sustained by British craft. While the destroyers all maintained their station without serious damage, the crew of the *Arethusa* began to more fully communicate to Tyrwhitt the particulars of the fairly heavy damage to his flagship. Most notable to the commodore upon the turn away from Heligoland was a loss in his ship's speed due to the hit suffered in the main feed tank. Tyrwhitt's flagship could not keep station with the other warships of the Harwich Force given the commodore's call for 20 knots. The commodore's chief engineer informed him that due to the damage, *Arethusa's* maximum speed was only 14 knots.

A final problem with the raid was the result of the Admiralty's not communicating to the operational commanders the last-minute reinforcement that had been attached to the operation. While Tyrwhitt was aware of the presence of both Goodenough's light cruisers and Beatty's battle cruisers, Commodore Keyes and his submarines remained ignorant, and this lack of information was a source of confusion in the battle. This problem first became apparent with radio messages picked up early in the battle by Goodenough from Tyrwhitt, informing that he was engaged with enemy forces. Goodenough, who at this point was eight miles to the northwest of Tyrwhitt with his six light cruisers, detached the *Nottingham* and the *Lowestoft* for support. These ships shaped a course southeast. Keyes, who was also to the north of Tyrwhitt with his flagship, the *Lurcher*, and the destroyer *Firedrake*, also received Tyrwhitt's messages and shaped a course toward the action. The two forces subsequently cruised into proximity of one another. Due to the fog, Keyes's lookouts did not sight the two British cruisers until all four ships were in relatively close quarters.

As he was unaware of the presence of any light cruisers other than Tyrwhitt's, and these he knew were south of him, Keyes thought that the *Nottingham* and the *Lowestoft* were enemy vessels of the *Karlsruhe*-class. Indeed, the silhouettes of the *Town*-class and *Karlsruhe*-class were very similar, each having two masts and four funnels. The distance was such that Keyes quickly had to weigh his options between launching a torpedo attack or fleeing from the cruisers. Fortune and good leadership benefited both Keyes and the captains of the two cruisers.

For his part, Keyes decided not to attack, which was fortunate because his destroyers might have torpedoed British vessels. Keyes reasoned that the light cruisers could easily destroy his ships before they could close to torpedo range. He also had some doubt as to their nationality in the minutes after the initial sighting, as the light cruisers did not engage him. This led Keyes to believe that perhaps the vessels were not enemies. The cruiser captains, on the other hand, were able to identify Keyes's destroyers as being British. Although visibility was low, the silhouettes of the *Lurcher* and the *Firedrake* did not match any German torpedo boat. Even so, this turn of events did not mean that Goodenough's cruisers were out of danger. Keyes, as he was not completely sure of their nationality, consequently decided to shadow them.[44] In addition, even if Keyes did positively identify them, the submarines of his force would still be unaware of the presence of additional British cruisers in the bight and might attack them. The possibility of British ships being sunk by friendly fire remained.

Confusion also reigned for Tyrwhitt, although to a lesser extent than Keyes, in the wake of his turn west. Keyes had duly reported to Tyrwhitt the presence of two enemy light cruisers northwest of his position. Such a report was a source of concern for Tyrwhitt. Although Tyrwhitt knew of the presence of Goodenough and suspected that Keyes had actually spotted vessels under Goodenough's command, he could not establish for certain from the wireless message whether the craft Keyes spotted were British or German. Also, Tyrwhitt found his force remaining disorganized due to a fresh encounter with a German warship.

This encounter, which began to unfold even before Tyrwhitt made his turn west, proved to be the one mitigation of the overall unfavorable situation of the raid. Goodenough's dispatch of the *Nottingham* and the *Lowestoft* to the battle site led them toward the lone German torpedo boat V-187 under the command of Lieutenant Commander Lechler. This craft was the leader of Torpedo Boat Flotilla I under the overall command of Commander Wallis. After trying to make contact with G-194 in the opening minutes of the raid into Heligoland Bight, Lechler had pursued a course east-southeast that placed him in the middle of the British forces in the area. At 8:00 A.M., he sighted what he believed to be two armored cruisers and tried to report their presence to the German high command. British jamming, however, prevented the receipt of this message. The same efforts by the British, in addition to the overall unsatisfactory communication of the Germans that hindered the speedy transmission of messages, resulted in Lechler's and Wallis's not knowing any information concerning British force strength other than what they had reported. This problem proved a critical one. The two officers were aware only of the armored cruisers, which they could outrun because of the generally superior speed of their vessel. They therefore tried to maintain contact with the cruisers that they sighted rather than making a course immediately for Heligoland Island. They certainly would have pursued the latter course had they known of the German reports concerning large numbers of enemy destroyers with speed that matched that of the German vessel. Lechler did not actually shape a course for Heligoland until at 8:20 A.M. he received a message from Maas, which had first been issued ten minutes earlier, for all craft of both torpedo boat flotillas to retreat under the guns of Heligoland in the face of the raid.[45] These few precious minutes proved critical. By the time this message was received, the Harwich Force was engaging the light cruisers *Stettin* and *Frauenlob*, with Tyrwhitt's forces steaming in a course roughly south. Unbeknownst to Lechler and Wallis, this placed the British craft between V-187 and the safe haven of Heligoland. The forces under Blunt that lay slightly farther north of Tyrwhitt compounded the problem, as V-187 steamed toward potential disaster.

Lechler and Wallis began to gain an appreciation of their predicament almost at the same time that they received Maas's message to proceed to Heligoland. Blunt with the First Flotilla sighted the German ship through the mists at a range of six thousand yards. Captain Blunt dispatched the Fifth Division of his flotilla, comprising *Goshawk*, *Lizard*, *Lapwing*, and *Phoenix*, in pursuit of the lone German craft. He soon thereafter believed that the destroyer might in fact be Keyes in the *Lurcher*, as he was aware of the commodore's presence in the area. Although Blunt tried to recall the destroyers, Captain Meade in the *Goshawk*, the division leader, ignored the order. Being closer to the German craft than Blunt, Meade could clearly distinguish it as an enemy vessel. As the British ships bore down on them off their port bow, Lechler and Wallis immediately shaped a course south toward the Jade River while signaling the engine room for full speed to make the dash to safety.

There was certainly the possibility that V-187 might escape. On the surface, the German vessel enjoyed a full 5-knot advantage in speed over its British pursuers. Even so, the attainment of maximum speed took some time, in which the British closed the range. In addition, the southern course allowed the British to get nearer to their enemy, as Blunt's ships approached V-187 on a course south-southeast. These facts led Lechler and Wallis to further alter the course of their ship to the southwest to try to make either the Jade or the Ems River. The need for this correction was great given the opening of British fire on their craft. These shots, however, were not accurate. The crew of V-187 observed that only one gun had a general fix on their range. Shells from this piece sailed over the bridge, but caused no damage.[46] Amidst intermittent fire from the British destroyers, V-187's guns remained silent. At first, the enemy's range exceeded that of the guns of the German craft, owing to the smaller caliber shipped by German torpedo boats in general. Once the distance closed to 5,250 yards, however, V-187 answered the fire with its stern 3.45-inch gun.

Lechler and Wallis's situation did not remain very favorable for long, as the threat to V-187 increased greatly when two British light cruisers appeared through the mists to the northwest on a course toward their ship. These proved to be the *Lowestoft* and the *Nottingham,* which Goodenough earlier had detached from his force. At first, the Germans believed that these two were their own ships, because V-187's signalman mistook a searchlight signal from one of the light cruisers for a German recognition signal. In fact, this British signal was issued to try to clearly establish the identity of the German ship. When the British were satisfied that the craft in view was enemy, they opened fire at a range of four thousand yards. Lechler and Wallis directed the forward 3.45-inch gun to answer the light cruiser fire, but the situation was now rather poor for the Germans. Torpedo boat V-187 faced four destroyers and two light cruisers. Each of the latter vastly outgunned the German ship as they possessed nine 6-inch guns in their main battery as opposed to the two 3.45-inch guns of the torpedo boat. These vessels consequently outranged V-187, making escape all the more difficult. Even if V-187 outdistanced the light cruisers, as the craft had roughly a 7-knot advantage over them, it would still be in range for some time. The gravity of the situation became clearer as the ship suffered its first hit. All members of the crew, with the exception of the boiler stokers, subsequently were ordered to equip themselves with life jackets and firearms.

Lechler and Wallis at this point realized that only bold action could save their vessel. Wallis ordered a turn to port on a course northeast in an effort to steam straight through the destroyers of Fifth Division and reach Heligoland. The center torpedo tube of V-187 was trained to starboard and the depth setting on the weapon set to three feet, while the guns remained ready for action. The five ships subsequently engaged in a brief battle. The strategy seemed to succeed, as the action surprised the British commanders as well as their crews. In addition, British fire temporarily halted as the gun crews lost the range to the German ship. Torpedo-boat V-187 sped virtually unscathed through the Fifth Division and cruised unmolested past them for a further 2,200 yards on its dash to Heligoland. The hopes for the Germans vanished at this point with the appearance of the four British destroyers in Third Division, First Flotilla. The other two divisions of the flotilla lay nearby in what amounted to a barrier of destroyers that blocked the path to Heligoland. These ships opened fire on V-187 while those of Fifth Division reversed course northward. The German craft found itself sandwiched between eight destroyers and blanketed in a hail of shells from two directions.

Torpedo boat V-187 had no chance in these circumstances. The first hit greatly reduced the ship's offensive capability as a shell penetrated the hull close to the forward 3.45-inch gun. The explosion below decks killed most of the gun crew and reduced the performance of the gun to only sporadic fire for the rest of the engagement. Another shell tore through the hull and exploded in Number 4 fire room, reducing the propulsion power of the ship. Further shells hit the bridge, destroyed all of the boilers, and put the forward turbine out of action. The damage to the propulsion machinery of V-187 produced steam and black smoke that poured out of the hatch and skylight located over the engines and boilers. This greatly hampered the aft gun crew's efforts to inflict some damage on their British tormentors. Indeed, at this point most of the ship was shrouded in smoke as a result of the steam and smoke aft and a large fire on the bow that resulted from the hit to the forward gun.

Despite the damage, the Germans were not willing to surrender. The hit to the bridge seriously wounded Lieutenant Commander Lechler and killed the helmsman, but Wallis, also wounded, endeavored to continue the fight. He placed Lieutenant Jasper in command of the ship and gave orders to him accordingly, but the efforts did not produce any result and led Wallis to give up resistance:

> I gave him orders to have explosive charges [to scuttle the ship] ready and I myself took the rudder, as it was not manned and since it was very difficult to make orders understood, for the purpose of ramming the last destroyer in the enemy line. The rudder could not be put hard over and there I received a report that the ammunition was expended and thereupon gave the order to place the explosive charges in the compartments designated in the general quarters bill. I received orders that the charges were placed. Lieutenant Jasper had the word passed in all compartments. I threw the secret books on the bridge overboard and gave the order to abandon ship.[47]

The order to abandon ship, however, had not been received by all, including Lieutenant Friedrich Braune in command of the aft gun. Despite the report to Wallis of the contrary, Braune still had some rounds left for his piece. The British, believing that the contest was largely over, were calling on Wallis to surrender while keeping up an intermittent fire and closing on the German ship to rescue survivors. At this point, a round from Braune's gun tore through the hull of the destroyer *Goshawk* from a range of only four hundred yards. The shell exploded in the vessel's wardroom and caused significant damage. In response, the British destroyers resumed heavier fire on the German torpedo boat.

British shells subsequently destroyed the aft gun, but neither that damage or that caused by the numerable hits before accounted for the end of V-187. The account of Lieutenant Jasper provides the context for the last moments of the ship: "The ship had little way on and was listing to port. . . . I took one of the four explosive charges that were on the bridge, set it, and threw it in the forward turbine room. The bridge personnel put two others in the forward part of the ship. . . . After fixing up the charges I gave orders to leave the ship on the leeside of the firing. . . . I jumped overboard just before (according to my calculations) the charges would take effect."[48] At 9:10 A.M., the detonation of the scuttling charges led to the sinking of V-187 by the bow with its flag still flying.

The destroyer *Defender* as well as the other seven craft in the two divisions of the First Flotilla endeavored to rescue the survivors of the German torpedo boat through launching boats to pick up the stricken crew. This process began even before *V-187* sank, as according to Lieutenant Jasper he was already in a British lifeboat at the time of the vessel's loss.[49] The appearance of the light cruiser *Stettin*, however, forced them to interrupt the operation after only some eight minutes. Commander Nerger reappeared on the scene of battle after rais- ing full steam in his ship's boilers (the lack of which was part of the reason why he had broken off the engagement with the *Fearless*). The return of the *Stettin* was prompted by wireless reports received by Nerger at 8:30 A.M., which re- vealed that the vessels composing the western portion of the outer patrol line were being attacked by enemy ships. Nerger cruised toward the position of the harassed German craft, and at about 9:00 A.M. sighted light smoke clouds off his starboard bow that proved to be the British destroyers in the process of finishing off *V-187*. Commander Nerger was able six minutes later to see "eight destroy- ers bunched together. I at once signaled the Admiral Commanding Scouting Forces, 'Am in action with flotilla in square 133,' turned to port and opened fire at 7,200 metres. The first salvo straddled and thereafter many hits were ob- served. While most of the destroyers scattered, two remained on the spot, appar- ently badly damaged."[50] In fact, these two craft were not badly damaged British ships. One of them was the *Defender*, whose crew was trying desperately to get boats, men, and the German survivors back on board while under fire. The other craft was most likely *V-187* itself. Nerger reported that he opened fire on the British destroyers at 9:06 A.M., which was four minutes before the scuttling charges sent *V-187* to the bottom. The efforts of the *Defender* did not prove en- tirely successful. As the *Stettin* bore down on the position of the British de- stroyer, the commander was forced to abandon two of his whaler boats and ten crewmembers manning them in order to save his ship.

Nerger was completely unaware of the rescue operation as he engaged the British, which is clear in many instances through his after-action report. The resulting engagement produced little gain for either side. The destroyer *Ferret* fired a torpedo that missed, and the *Stettin* was hit three times. One of these shots hit the rigging that contained the wireless lines, thus putting the radio out of action until 11:00 A.M., and also damaged the ship's aft funnel. Another shot hit the ammunition of Number 3 gun on the starboard side and caused a fire with no appreciable damage. The last shell hit the hull below the waterline, but did not penetrate or cause any flooding. The German ship suffered two dead and nine wounded personnel. In return, the *Stettin's* inaccurate fire, consisting of only four salvoes, inflicted no appreciable damage on the fleeing British craft. Even so, Nerger was convinced that his action had either seriously dam- aged or sunk at least one British vessel, as he pointed out the sighting of five empty cutters, a number of dinghies, cork lifebelts, life buoys, and sundry other objects.[51] Oftentimes, the presence of such debris is attributable to the sinking of a ship, but in this case it represented primarily the equipment that the col- lection of British destroyers were forced to leave behind. Some of it may also have been debris from the sinking of V-187 minutes before Nerger arrived at the position where it foundered. German lookouts on the *Stettin* never saw the British crewmen who remained behind in the two abandoned boats from the *Defender*, as Nerger tried to pursue the British destroyers and passed by the position where V-187 sank. Rather than being a captain guilty of inhumanity in the face of an act of mercy, as members of the British press later asserted, Nerger felt that he had acted appropriately and had inflicted loss on the enemy when he broke off his pursuit to repair his ship. At 9:13 A.M., Nerger broke off the action because the British destroyers had vanished from sight. After having made some repairs, at 9:30 A.M., Nerger shaped a course northeast toward the vicinity of Heligoland.

Upon his doing so, the Germans left the vicinity of the abandoned boats from the *Defender* as well as the German survivors of V-187 who had not been picked up. Fortunately for them, the sinking of V-187, the arrival of the *Stettin*, and subsequent events were observed by Lieutenant Commander Ernest W. Leir, who was in command of British submarine E-4 as part of the inner force of submarines charged with patrolling the area of Heligoland. Leir tried to attack the *Stettin* as it approached the British destroyers, but the German light cruiser had altered course before he could get his craft within torpedo range. Leir decided afterward to wait until the *Stettin* left the vicinity, and around 9:30 A.M. he surfaced near the abandoned British whaler boats. Leir learned that the boats contained one British officer and nine men from the *Defender*, two officers and eight men of V-187 whom Leir later classed as "unwounded," and 18 wounded officers and ratings.[52] Leir could not embark all of these people onto his relatively small boat. Indeed, its crew complement consisted of only thirty officers and men. As a result, the lieutenant commander decided to take aboard the British seamen as well as three Germans—two officers and one rating. Leir left the majority of the wounded in the British boats under the charge of the unwounded German men. He issued them with water, biscuit, and a compass with which to make the voyage back to Heligoland. In addition to the men that Leir left behind, and unbeknownst to him, were five more survivors in an additional boat. The survivors of V-187, now in three boats, were later rescued by two torpedo boats of Torpedo Boat Flotilla V. After reaching Heligoland, these ships and three others were again dispatched to locate and bring in any German small craft still in the bight. Three of these, V-3, G-7, and G-10, aided the *Frauenlob* in its efforts to tow T-33 to safety. The other two, G-9 and G-11, cruised to the southwest. Once they reached the southern boundary of the original patrol line, the two craft turned northward and at 11:00 A.M. sighted the German survivors and recovered them.

The sinking of V-187 proved to be the only gain for the British after two hours and thirteen minutes of contact with the Germans. The only other opportunity that could have presented itself was an engagement with the light cruiser *Hela*, but this proved stillborn. Captain Paul Wolfram, upon hearing reports of action in Heligoland Bight, had proceeded from his patrol position, but reversed while fifteen miles southwest of Heligoland upon hearing that the enemy had turned southwest away from the island. Wolfram's decision was certainly a fortuitous one, as the British could easily have destroyed his ship. Built in 1896, it was little more than a museum piece, being far too obsolete for a battle against modern units. The German official history of the war at sea in World War I concluded that the opening hours of the British raid could "scarcely have come up to the expectations of the British. . . . [T]he attacker was forced to quit the field due to the fire effect of the materially, as well as numerically, far inferior German cruisers."[53] While the contention that the fire of the German cruisers led the British to turn westward is somewhat erroneous, as only the *Arethusa* was significantly damaged, and attributable to bias, the former assertion was entirely correct. Up to 9:10 A.M., with the sinking of V-187, the Germans had largely held their own, and the raid could be classed more of a failure than a success in terms of its mission.

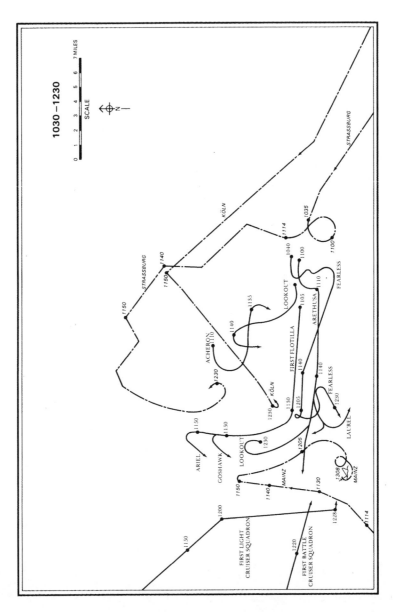

Fig. 3. Phase 2. Reproduced through the kind permission of the Naval Institute Press.

CHAPTER FOUR

THE BATTLE OF THE BIGHT BECOMES A DECISIVE VICTORY

T HE SITUATION FOR BRITISH FORCES in Heligoland Bight in the minutes following the sinking of V-187 was largely unfavorable despite the fleeting triumph over the German torpedo boat. While V-187 met its end, Tyrwhitt tried to consolidate the forces under his command and assess his overall position in terms of the battle. Confusion continued to be the order of the day as British commanders continued to receive erroneous reports that Keyes had sighted enemy cruisers in his vicinity. Such false information hampered the efforts of all British commanders in battle, as they did not have an accurate understanding of events in the combat zone with which to make the most appropriate decisions.

Goodenough's actions, which unfolded almost simultaneously with fire being opened on V-187, exacerbated this condition in the wake of Keyes's sighting the light cruisers *Lowestoft* and *Nottingham* of his force. Just to the north of Keyes, Goodenough tried to decide whether Keyes had indeed sighted enemy cruisers rather than his own and also sought to fix firmly Keyes's position; at this time the radio transmissions from Keyes placed him in an area other than where Goodenough believed him to be. While Goodenough sought to make sense of Keyes's transmissions, he proceeded at 20 knots with his four light cruisers on a southwest course toward Heligoland in preparation to make the

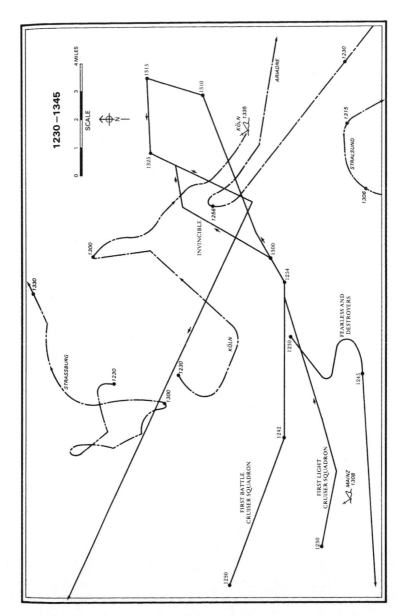

Fig. 4. Phase 3. *Reproduced through the kind permission of the Naval Institute Press.*

sweep west with Tyrwhitt. It was this action that brought him closer to Keyes. At 8:25 A.M., through the mist Goodenough's force spotted the silhouettes of two destroyers that the lookouts could not identify. These vessels proved to be Keyes's *Lurcher* and the *Firedrake*, which at this time were on a course toward the sound of the guns from the engagement with *V-187*. Keyes did not sight Goodenough's cruisers until shortly after 8:40 A.M., and his response once again flirted with disaster. The commodore believed that the four cruisers were the original two he had sighted earlier along with two additional reinforcements. He subsequently altered course northwest to try to draw the supposed enemy ships toward Moore's supporting battle cruisers.

This encounter disrupted the movements of the raid overall, as Goodenough had been steaming into a position to make his sweep westward to support Tyrwhitt. Now, he shelved this plan following a message at 9:45 A.M. from Keyes that stated he was being chased by four light cruisers. Tyrwhitt three minutes later decided to ask Goodenough to support Keyes: "Please chase westward. . . . Commodore (S) is being chased by four light cruisers."[1] As Goodenough hauled off toward Keyes's position, he had no idea that in fact he was pursuing his own ships. This situation did not last long. Only minutes after his report did Keyes begin to sense that something was wrong. As he cruised farther out to sea, the mist that lay over the bight began to dissipate, and Keyes could see that each cruiser had four funnels and two masts. He sensed that the craft could be British and decided at 9:50 A.M. to issue a challenge by searchlight to them. Goodenough in his flagship *Southampton* made the appropriate response. Both British commanders now closed one another.

While Keyes was probably pleased at the resolution of this episode, he certainly felt great concern over the situation. He had no way of informing his submarines of the presence of Goodenough's forces, which meant that the British submarines might torpedo their own vessels. Keyes's frustration over the entire lack of coordination from the Admiralty showed itself in this message from Keyes to Goodenough: "I was not informed that you were coming into the area; you run great risk from our submarines. . . . Your unexpected appearance has upset all our plans. There are submarines off Ems."[2] Goodenough's response both typified the confusion surrounding the situation and revealed that he too appreciated the gravity of it. The commodore's signal read: "I came under detailed orders. I am astonished that you were not told. I have signaled to *Lion* that we should withdraw. *Nottingham* and *Lowestoft* are somewhere in the vicinity."[3] The latter part of Goodenough's response refers to a signal he made to Beatty. At 10:10 A.M., Beatty aboard the *Lion* received a message that read "Commodores (S) and (T) had no knowledge of 1 L.C.S. (First Light Cruiser Squadron) taking part. I consider we should withdraw at once."[4] Beatty does not seem to have acted on Goodenough's advice. Rather, he continued to hold his position northwest of Heligoland.

Even so, both Keyes and Goodenough were entirely justified in their concern over the situation. Goodenough's reaction to learning of Keyes in the area rested in part on events prior to the meeting, when he did indeed encounter *E-6* of the force ordered to act as decoys to lure German vessels away from Heligoland toward British surface forces. Goodenough at around 9:30 A.M. had sighted the periscope of this boat, under the command of Lieutenant Commander C. P. Talbot, and had made efforts to ram what he thought was an enemy submarine. Talbot ordered his crew to submerge the craft deeper and thus avoided the keel of Goodenough's flagship. Even so, like Goodenough he believed that the opposing craft was a legitimate target. The lieutenant commander had noted that the light cruiser shipped four funnels and two masts. In keeping with Keyes's pre-battle instructions, Talbot believed that the cruiser was a German warship. A second potential disaster was avoided only due to the British commander's presence of mind. Talbot had two occasions where he was in proximity to Goodenough's flagship. On one of these, he maneuvered for a torpedo attack and only called it off when he was able to see the cross of St. George in the ensign of the *Southampton*. The fact that Talbot could make this visual identification of such a relatively small object is testimony to the very close range of his intended target and how narrowly the *Southampton* avoided being sunk.[5] Had this happened, the fault certainly would have lain with the actions of the Admiralty in the opening hours of the operation.

The British high command's mistake endangered not only Goodenough's light cruisers, but also Beatty's battle cruisers, of which the submarines were equally unaware. In addition, while the immediate source of confusion vanished for Goodenough, Keyes, and by extension the other commanders, its ramifications continued to disrupt the raid. Unfortunately for the British, Keyes neglected to tell Tyrwhitt that the "enemy cruisers" were indeed those of Goodenough. A little after 9:50 A.M., Tyrwhitt as a result altered the course of his own force eastward toward Keyes in the hope of aiding him, despite the fact that by this time the damage suffered earlier by *Arethusa* had decreased the speed of his flagship to 10 knots. While he changed course, the commodore caught a brief glimpse of the *Stettin*, and Blunt in the *Fearless* tried to engage, but the action ended quickly when the German ship disappeared in the mist. By this time, Tyrwhitt's earlier suspicions that Keyes was in contact with British light cruisers rather than German prompted him to stop most of his forces. To confirm his suspicion, the commodore sent Third Flotilla under Commander Arthur Dutton toward Keyes's position to confirm his belief that all was actually fine for his friend.

While Dutton pursued his mission, Tyrwhitt in the *Arethusa* and Blunt in the *Fearless* with the First Flotilla closed one another until at 10:17 A.M. the two commanders were in semaphore range and brought their ships to a stop in order to communicate. Tyrwhitt's engine room crew used the next twenty minutes to

effect repairs to the flagship's propulsion system and weaponry. Amidst these repairs, Tyrwhitt and Blunt apprised one another fully of all information concerning the actions that unfolded in the raid. Tyrwhitt learned about the destruction
of V-187 only at this time. At the close of this exchange, the engine room of
Arethusa reported that the ship was again capable of 20 knots and that all guns
save two of the 4-inch pieces were in working order. At 10:39 A.M., Tyrwhitt consequently ordered a resumption of the sweep west. By this time, the Third Flotilla was already back on the westward sweep once it had established that all was
well with Keyes. Tyrwhitt now put the rest of the force back on the westward
course and ordered Blunt to assume a position slightly ahead of Arethusa and
keep sight of the flagship in the event that the hastily made repairs to the ship's
feed tank failed and again cut the vessel's speed. Tyrwhitt not only wanted to
gain greater distance from Heligoland, which he had closed again in trying to
help Keyes, but also knew full well that he lay in relative proximity to the
mouths of the rivers that housed Germany's North Sea naval bases and that a
response by the German navy must be under way.

Tyrwhitt was correct, but the response would not comprise heavy ships such
as battleships and battle cruisers as the Germans suffered from problems inherent in their defense of the bight. Commander in chief of the High Seas Fleet
Admiral Friedrich von Ingenohl ordered Hipper at Wilhelmshaven to raise
steam in all his ships as early as 8:43 A.M. Even so, Ingenohl paused when Hipper transmitted "Will you permit Moltke and Von Der Tann to leave in support
as soon as it is clear?"[6] Only at 9:08 A.M. did Hipper receive a response, in which
Ingenohl said that the battle cruisers would be released only upon information
that revealed the full force strength of the enemy. The other battle cruiser of
Hipper's force, his flagship Seydlitz, and the armored cruiser Blucher did not
enter the exchange. Only the starboard engine of the former was operational
because of work being done on the condenser of the port side machinery. The
latter ship lay just off Wilhelmshaven in order to re-coal. None of this, however,
really mattered at the time as the discussion proved an academic one. The passage of German ships from Wilhelmshaven to the Jade Bar that lay at the
mouth of the river took a full hour. This inability to react quickly meant that
the battle could well be over before heavy units could arrive in the area of Heligoland. More important, however, was the fact that because of the tides, the
ships could not even cross the Jade Bar for several hours after the exchange between Hipper and Ingenohl. On 28 August, the tide was particularly low, with
absolute low tide being reached at 9:33 A.M. with a depth of some twenty-five
feet. The hulls of the battle cruisers all drew more water than this and would
consequently ground and possibly damage themselves if the attempt was made.
For example, the hulls of both the Moltke and the Von Der Tann had a draft of
over twenty-six feet. The larger battleships in Wilhelmshaven, numbering
eleven either anchored off the port or in the installation itself, were in a similar

position if ordered to sortie. After the initial report of combat in the bight, these vessels had been ordered to raise steam for a possible engagement, but Ingenohl never issued a general order for the entire High Seas Fleet to prepare for battle. As a consequence of geography, the High Seas Fleet could not cross the Jade Bar between 7:00 A.M. and 12:00 A.M. on the day of the raid.[7] Effectively, the High Seas Fleet was bottled up by the limitations of its own anchorage and was incapable of a response.

This geographic problem did not hinder some heavy units of the High Seas Fleet, but even these did not participate in the battle. The battleships *Helgoland* and *Thuringen* were in position to aid as they were outside the Jade Bar. Even so, sailors who heard the distant sound of gunfire would be sorely disappointed at unfolding events. One crewman on board *Helgoland* wrote of the situation: "'Battle stations! Clear the decks for action!' came the order at 9:30. 'Stretcher bearers in front of the sick bay. At last! At last! At last!'" This enthusiasm did not last long. The same crewman subsequently wrote that "August 28th was a black day for the crew of the *Helgoland*. . . . A few miles away from us our ships were in the midst of a heavy fight. We didn't know the size of the ships involved. . . . Then on top of all that we got orders to drop anchor at once. . . . Needless to say, we were immensely disappointed by this order."[8] Ingenohl not only did not issue a general order for the High Seas Fleet to prepare for battle, but he also held back those units that were already in combat readiness in keeping with his earlier order to Hipper on the use of his battle cruisers.

The absence of battleships and battle cruisers, however, did not signal a lack of response by the German Navy to the British raid. By the time that discussions were under way on the use of Hipper's ships, efforts were well in motion for the deployment of the myriad of light cruisers that lay in the vicinity of the bight. For these vessels, draft did not present a problem. An example is the *Köln*, flagship of commander Second Scouting Group and senior officer of torpedo-boats Rear Admiral Leberecht Maas. This ship drew 17' 7" of water as opposed to over 26' for larger battleships and battle cruisers. The *Köln* had retired to Wilhelmshaven from its patrol station in the bight on 27 August in order to coal. On the morning of the battle, four other light cruisers also lay in the Wilhelmshaven area: *Strassburg*, *Stralsund*, *Rostock*, and *Kolberg*. The light cruiser *Ariadne* also lay nearby in its patrol position near Wangerooge at the mouth of the Jade River as a unit of the bight defense. The light cruiser *Mainz* augmented the power of the vessels at Wilhelmshaven. Under the command of Captain Wilhelm Pasche, it lay at the mouth of the Ems River. Finally, the light cruisers *Danzig* and *München* were anchored at Brunsbüttel, near the North Sea entry to the Kiel Canal that led to the Baltic Sea. These nine light cruisers, in addition to the *Stettin* and the *Frauenlob*, made up a powerful force and a significant threat to the British.

At 7:35 A.M., Hipper began to issue orders to Maas and the other light cruisers when he directed the *Köln* and the *Strassburg* to sail in support of the bight patrol that was under attack. A similar order went out to Captain Pasche in the *Mainz*, while the light cruisers *Stralsund, Danzig,* and *München* received orders to make ready for sea. Maas in the *Köln* and the *Strassburg* were the first to sea as at 9:34 A.M. they passed the Jade lightship and shaped a course westnorthwest in search of British units. Pasche put to sea almost a half hour later, despite having made preparations to sortie as much as an hour earlier. Heavy fog over the Ems River impeded his progress out into the bight. Even so, by 10:00 A.M., three more light cruisers were en route to Tyrwhitt, while many more prepared for action.

The deployment of German reinforcements, however, greatly detracted from their offensive potential. Maas chose not to concentrate his light cruisers before proceeding into Heligoland Bight. The German official history as well as some naval accounts of the battle attribute this fact in part to Maas's offensive spirit. Maas certainly had more than the basic desire to engage the enemy driving his decision not to wait and mass his ships. The rear admiral not only wanted to attack as quickly as possible, but felt that it was safe to do so given the battle reports that specified the presence of a few light cruisers and destroyers. He certainly was not aware of the presence of either Goodenough's light cruisers or Beatty's battle cruisers. A faulty presumption about the weather in the bight contributed to Maas's belief that he could safely attack piecemeal. The weather around Wilhelmshaven was relatively clear with good visibility, as opposed to the fog in Heligoland Bight. Neither the units of the patrol, the garrison on Heligoland, nor the German high command had informed Maas of poor weather. Maas consequently steamed into the bight with fragmentary information that contributed to his decision. Captain Pasche sortied with the same poor information, being told simply to "attack in rear enemy torpedo boat flotilla near Heligoland."[9] Consequently, the three light cruisers all steamed on different courses into the bight. Based on the last sighting report of the British, the rear admiral believed that his enemy was retiring northwest. He decided to shape a course northwest in the *Köln* directly for the last known position of the British, to attack them in the rear. In the meantime, the *Strassburg* pursued a course slightly farther south to the west-northwest to try to hit the retreating British in the flank of their formation. Captain Pasche in the *Mainz* approached the bight on a course northnortheast to try to catch the British, pursuant of his specific orders to try to take the enemy in the rear. Each one of these ships faced the possibility of disaster through encountering, alone, large numbers of enemy vessels in much the same way that V-187 met its end. The decision to go into battle piecemeal would exact a heavy price on the German Navy.

The first to encounter this situation was the *Strassburg* under the command of Captain Retzmann. At 10:55 A.M. the German light cruiser was steaming through the mist in the bight when its lookouts spotted two cruisers and between ten and twelve destroyers. These proved to be a portion of the Harwich Force that comprised the *Arethusa*, the *Fearless*, and the First Flotilla. At roughly the same time, Tyrwhitt sighted the approaching German warship and subsequently ordered a turn to the southwest. The commodore identified the enemy vessel and realized that it outgunned his flagship. This conviction seemed confirmed when the *Strassburg* opened fire on the *Arethusa* at a range of some 9,000 yards and on its third salvo achieved a straddle, although no shells hit the British flagship. Tyrwhitt responded to this situation when he ordered Blunt and the First Flotilla to execute a torpedo attack. Retzmann shifted fire to the approaching destroyers, but it was inaccurate. Nevertheless, several shells got quite close to the approaching British craft. The commander of the *Hind*, another of the destroyers in the First Division, noted that as his men prepared the torpedo tubes amidst the singing of a song called "Get Out and Get Under," one man had his hat blown overboard by the displacement of air from a German salvo that passed just astern.[10] Amidst the fire, Commander Morey of the *Acheron* led the attack as the First Division, First Flotilla, launched seven torpedoes at a range of some 4,500 yards. All missed when Retzmann turned to port to avoid them, but as he did so he lost sight on the British vessels. At the moment, he chose not to reengage in light of the threat of torpedo attack. Tyrwhitt subsequently recalled the First Division because not only did he want to continue west, but he also did not want the destroyers to engage heavier ships in a pitched battle. As a result, the first engagement with the *Strassburg* was over.

The turning of the *Strassburg*, however, provided no respite for the British as the other German light cruisers closed on their position. As Blunt and the First Flotilla turned back onto their westward course, they sighted another German light cruiser, which proved to be the *Köln*, steaming toward them from the southeast. Another short but pitched engagement much like that with the *Strassburg* ensued; like the former contest, it resulted in the German ship's retreating in the face of large numbers of enemy torpedo craft, while Tyrwhitt again broke off the action to continue west once more. The one telling outcome of the contest was the fact that Tyrwhitt believed his situation had deteriorated greatly through the arrival of heavy units of the German High Seas Fleet. Tyrwhitt mistakenly identified the *Köln* as an armored cruiser of the *Roon*-class, which was a significantly more powerful vessel than one of the German light cruisers and easily outgunned the British cruisers. The German armored cruiser *Roon* mounted four 8.3-inch guns that could destroy the British ships from a range that the British, with their smaller caliber guns, could not reach. Such a vessel also shipped ten 6-inch guns.[11] The largest guns of the Harwich Force were the *Arethusa's* two 6-inch guns. The commodore was convinced at this point that he needed the aid of the supporting craft that lay to the north. He sent two wireless messages in quick succession to Beatty to this effect. The first read, "Am attacked by a large cruiser 54 degrees, 0 minutes North, 7 degrees, 12 minutes East," while the second stated, "Respectfully request that I may be supported. Am hard pressed."[12] Beatty's response was to order Good-enough to detach two more of his light cruisers to assist Tyrwhitt. Goodenough decided instead to shape a course toward Tyrwhitt at a speed of 25 knots with all four of his vessels. The light cruisers *Nottingham* and *Lowestoft* were unavailable as they had failed to regain Goodenough after being detached earlier. They consequently took no further part in the battle. While Goodenough proceeded south, Beatty was left to debate whether to risk the battle cruisers through a sortie into the bight. Even so, the British situation showed promise of improvement given the potential augmentation of Tyrwhitt's force by Goodenough's light cruisers.

The need for these ships became more pressing with the reappearance of the *Strassburg*, which was steaming on a course northwest. Captain Retzmann, following the initial contest between his ship and the British, did not wish to disengage completely despite the fact that he faced large numbers of enemy vessels. Rather, the German captain had turned to follow the British destroyers as they resumed their westward sweep. The gunfire from the German vessel seemed quite intense to Tyrwhitt: "We received a very severe and most accurate fire from this cruiser. Salvo after salvo was falling between twenty and thirty yards short, but not a single shell struck; two torpedoes were also fired at us, being well directed, but fell short."[13] Tyrwhitt once again broke off his sweep west and steered a course west-northwest with Blunt and the First Flotilla. At the same time, the Third Flotilla, being farther west, reversed course to the sound of the guns. The ferocity of this action led to another call for help, this one from Blunt, who wired to Beatty at 11:30 A.M. the message "Assistance urgently required."[14] This action unfolded much like the previous two. Under Tyrwhitt's orders, at 11:35 A.M. the First and Second Divisions of the Third Flotilla and the First Division of the First Flotilla executed a torpedo attack. The assault of these twelve destroyers almost resulted in Retzmann's ship being hit twice. One torpedo passed on a parallel course to port of the ship, while another one passed astern. Although these missed, the *Strassburg* did suffer some damage from a 6-inch shell from the *Arethusa* that penetrated the cruiser's armored belt and flooded two compartments. Given the torpedo attacks and the damage from gunfire, Retzmann once again decided to withdraw and pursued a course south. He now hoped to shadow the British and meet up with the *Mainz*, which he knew was approaching the area on a roughly northeasterly course.

Unlike the other contests, this one, although inconclusive, did result in a decision on the part of Beatty that proved decisive for the battle overall. As the second battle with the *Strassburg* unfolded, Beatty was in the process of deciding whether or not to employ the battle cruisers. The message from Blunt heightened the urgency of the matter and led to a discussion between himself and Captain Ernle Chatfield, the commander of the *Lion*, Beatty's flagship.

Chatfield in his autobiography captured the gravity of this decision through an outline of the situation as he and Beatty saw it:

> About noon on the 28th [actually a half an hour before] we intercepted a message from Tyrwhitt in the "Arethusa," which implied that he was in some difficulty and hotly engaged by German light cruisers. Beatty's force was then some forty miles north of Heligoland. The Bight was not a pleasant spot into which to take great ships; it was unknown whether mines had been laid there, submarines were sure to be on patrol, and to move into this area so near to the great German base at Wilhelmshaven was risky. Visibility was low, and to be surprised by a superior force of capital ships was not unlikely. They would have had plenty of time to leave harbor since Tyrwhitt's presence had first been known.[15]

Some of these considerations were not actually factors at about 11:30 A.M. when Beatty began to receive Tyrwhitt's messages. By this time, Hipper had issued orders that all German submarines be withdrawn from the bight as he wished to avoid the possibility of one of these craft mistaking any of the German light cruisers for the enemy and torpedoing them. In addition, at this time heavy German capital ships still could not cross the Jade Bar because of the tide. It is true that around 12:00 P.M. the depth of the water would be sufficient, but even then it would have taken time for the heavy units to actually maneuver into the bight. Nevertheless, Beatty faced a difficult decision given the factors outlined by Chatfield. According to the captain, however, Beatty was "not long in making up his mind. He said to me, 'What do you think we should do? I ought to go and support Tyrwhitt, but if I lose one of these valuable ships, the country will never forgive me.'" Chatfield responded, "Surely we must go," which led Beatty to make his decision to support Tyrwhitt with the battle cruisers.[16] Beatty reasoned that the factors against his participation were not significant enough to preclude his participation. In terms of enemy submarines, Beatty believed that the high speed of his ships dashing into the bight would make a torpedo attack impossible. He also suspected that—in part again due to the high speed of his ships—an enemy battle squadron could not get out of Wilhelmshaven quickly enough to prevent his ships from effectively supporting Tyrwitt.[17] At 11:35 A.M., Beatty consequently brought his three battle cruisers and those of Moore into a line ahead formation and steamed at a speed of 26 knots on a course southeast into the bight. Ten minutes later, he increased speed to 27 knots and steered to a course east-southeast. As he did so, Beatty transmitted via wireless to Blunt, the sender of the last call for assistance, "Am proceeding to your support."[18]

As Beatty made his decision and the contest with the *Strassburg* continued, the arrival of the third light cruiser, the *Mainz*, created still greater need for additional support for the British. The Second, Third, and Fifth Divisions of the

First Flotilla, those not involved in the action with *Strassburg* and positioned farther west, sighted the *Mainz* at 11:30 A.M. on a course north. These eleven destroyers consequently steered north as well to bring their guns and torpedoes to bear. Over the course of the next few minutes, as the opposing sides steamed parallel to one another on a course north-northwest, the destroyers tried to launch a torpedo attack, but it was unsuccessful. The German vessel, on the other hand, gave accurate fire that repeatedly straddled the British craft. The situation was consequently a poor one for the British vessels.

Captain Pasche found himself in a relatively favorable position until 11:45 A.M., when lookouts on *Mainz* sighted heavy smoke clouds to the northwest. A few minutes later, the Germans sighted Goodenough's four light cruisers, which Beatty had sent earlier to aid Tyrwhitt, steaming out of the mist. Pasche knew he was vastly outgunned, as he faced twenty-seven 6-inch guns aboard the British cruisers, and immediately gave orders for a turn to starboard in order to reverse course and attempt to flee the British. Fortunately for the Germans, over the next few minutes the *Mainz* did not have to face the destroyers that moments before had been the principal opponents. These ships did not see the arrival of Goodenough and consequently continued to steam on their previous course, thus moving away from the battle. Nevertheless, Pasche was in serious trouble quickly as "[e]ven while turning the salvoes of the opponent struck in the vicinity and a little latter *Mainz* received the first hits on the poop and deck amidships."[19] The Germans returned fire, but it was inaccurate as Pasche raced at 25 knots on a course south-southwest toward the Ems River. Despite the inaccuracy of his gun crews, however, Pasche held out hope that he could reach safety, as his ship entered a fog bank and slowly lost the British pursuers. By 11:55 A.M., Pasche could recognize the presence of the British light cruiser only through the flash of their guns when fired.

Unfortunately for the Germans, Pasche's situation quickly deteriorated as the Harwich Force appeared to the east. Tyrwhitt's and Blunt's contest with the *Strassburg* had ended, and they were back on their westward course. The Germans found themselves confronted not only by Goodenough's light cruisers to the north, but now also by the light cruisers *Arethusa* and *Fearless* and twenty destroyers composing the First, Second, and Third Divisions of the Third Flotilla) and the First Division of the First Flotilla. The other divisions of the First Flotilla remained a bit further north after having turned around to reenter the action. Blunt in the *Fearless* opened fire as Tyrwhitt in the *Arethusa*, along with the First and Second Divisions of the Third Flotilla, shaped a course northwest. The Third and Fourth Divisions turned to the southwest. Despite now being vastly outnumbered, the gun crews of the *Mainz* acquitted themselves admirably in the opening minutes when the British destroyers launched a torpedo attack. The destroyer *Laurel*, the lead ship of Fourth Division, was struck by three shells as the ship fired two torpedoes. The first hit penetrated the hull and exploded in the engine room, which cut the main steam pipe that fed the engines and killed four men. The second shell hit close to the forward 4-inch gun and killed most of the gun crew. The third hit detonated cordite (propellant) at the amidships gun that destroyed the aft funnel. Splinters from this explosion hit the vessel's captain, Commander Rose, in both legs. All told, the *Laurel* suffered twenty-three officers and men killed or wounded. The ship, now shrouded in steam from its cut feed line and smoke from its damage, could only retreat at slow speed due to the loss of power from the hit in the engine room. The steam and smoke probably did much to save the ship from being destroyed. The destroyer *Lysander* under Lieutenant Commander Wakefield avoided damage, but the *Liberty* was not as fortunate. After firing torpedoes, this ship was hit by a shell at the bridge that felled the mast. The blast decapitated its captain, Lieutenant Commander Nigel Barttelot, and killed the ship's signal man. The vessel's second lieutenant assumed command and guided the ship out of harm's way. Lieutenant Commander Malcolm Goldsmith's ship, the *Laertes*, also suffered damage when it was hit by a salvo of shells. One destroyed the gun amidships. Another penetrated one of the boiler rooms. The detonation of this shell cut the supply of steam to the engines and left the *Laertes* dead in the water. A third hit destroyed the middle funnel of the ship, while the last exploded in the vessel's cabin flat. The situation of the *Laertes* was serious after these hits, as the loss of propulsion power left the ship motionless in the face of the German light cruiser and consequently an easy target. Even so, the engine room restored power, and the ship managed to leave the battle zone without further damage.

The success the Germans had against the destroyers, however, did not come without cost. The damage to the *Mainz* in the engagement with the British sealed the ship's fate. British gunfire proved accurate, and early in the contest the rudder of the ship jammed at 10 degrees right rudder. All attempts to free the rudder and restore steering proved unsuccessful, despite the fact that the vessel's damage-control parties found no damage to the steering machinery or controls. They therefore assumed that an underwater shell hit had bent the rudder itself. As a result, the *Mainz* could only cruise in an ever-increasing turn to starboard. In addition, the ship's speed was reduced as Pasche order the port turbine shut down at the same time as the rudder ceased to function. Both of these allowed time for Goodenough's light cruisers to catch up with their German adversary, meaning that the *Mainz* would soon face six light cruisers as well as the destroyers of the Harwich Force. It also left the ship vulnerable to the torpedo attack of the destroyers. By 12:20 P.M., gunfire had destroyed many of the ship's guns, and the upper deck was laid waste. Shell hits penetrated the hull and destroyed large portions of the warship's interior. They also caused further damage to the ship's machinery that reduced the capacity of the starboard side turbine to half capacity, which further reduced the overall speed of the ship. Lieutenant Commander Tholens, the first officer of the *Mainz*, described the grave scene: "[C]asualty had followed upon casualty on the *Mainz*. About 1:20 P.M. [12:20 Greenwich Mean Time] most of the guns and gun crews were already out of action. The decks were shot to pieces. The sending up of ammunition had come to a standstill, and more than once compartments under the armored deck had to be cleared on account of the danger from smoke and gas."[20] The situation was certainly a grave one.

It was in this greatly damaged state that the *Mainz* suffered one torpedo hit from the British destroyers that had attacked it. This torpedo, fired from the *Lydiard* of the Third Division, Third Flotilla, hit portside amidships in Number 4 stokehold. According to engineer officer Johannes Johannsen, the blast was devastating:

> The ship reared up, bent very perceptively, and rocked for a considerable time. Auxiliary lighting was extinguished. All glasses, which had not already been accounted for by shell impacts, broke. The electric lights became dimmer and finally went out altogether. Flashlights then provided the only illumination. The engines no longer turned over. The leak pendulum now indicated that the ship was slowly sinking forward. All efforts to determine where the leak was were fruitless, since no compartments answered. . . . The conning tower no longer answered.[21]

By the time that the *Mainz* began to settle in the water, still more damage ensued from the fire of Goodenough's light cruisers, which by the time of the torpedo hit had closed to a distance of six thousand yards. This fire proved devastating, as a British officer on the *Southampton* wrote: "We closed down on her, hitting with every salvo. She was a mass of yellow flame and smoke as the lyddite [being the type of shells] detonated along her length. Her two after funnels melted away and collapsed. Red glows, indicating internal fires, showed through gaping wounds in her side."[22] This account is entirely accurate. By the time the British ceased fire, the *Mainz* had endured between two hundred and three hundred hits. Its radio room was destroyed, the two after funnels were gone, the searchlights were shot away, there were very large holes in the deck from shell hits, and almost all the guns with their crews were out of action. The upper deck was a "wild confusion of ruins, fire, heat, and corpses, covered over with green and yellow products of explosion, which produced suffocating gasses."[23] The *Mainz*, although not having surrendered, was completely disabled and incapable of continuing the action. Goodenough fully appreciated this fact and at 12:25 P.M. ordered a cease fire to his ships. The rest of the British force did the same.

The primary reason why the ship had not surrendered was the destruction itself that hindered command of the ship. Upon the torpedo hit, Captain Pasche ordered that all hands should get their life vests and directed the crew to scuttle the ship. The transmission of this order, however, proved impossible because the torpedo hit knocked out the communication system except for voice tubes that fed from the conning tower to the torpedo room and a few other compartments. As a result, only part of the crew carried out the captain's order. In addition, a shell blast killed Pasche and his navigator moments after the order as they both stepped out of the conning tower. Lieutenant Commander Tholens, the executive officer, did not know of the captain's last order as he had not been in the conning tower. When he arrived to assume command, Tholens gave the order to continue firing, but this proved quite ineffectual given that only two of the starboard guns were still in action. The crew did launch one torpedo to port and two to starboard, but none of these found their mark. Finally, other officers informed Tholens of Pasche's command. Tholens subsequently carried out the order as best he could given the state of communication in the ship. The portside engine room crew opened the sea valves in the compartment, while other crewmen did the same in the torpedo room. Even then, however, not all of the crew were aware of the order. Many began making their way to the upper deck only after the British firing ceased, while many more remained trapped below decks due to a huge fire amidships that prevented their passage to safety.

Following the ceasefire order, three British vessels closed on the *Mainz* to try to rescue the survivors. These ships were the light cruiser *Liverpool* and the destroyers *Lurcher* and *Firedrake*. The *Liverpool* lowered boats to rescue survivors in the water as the latter two vessels, Keyes's ships, arrived upon the end of the engagement. Keyes himself in the *Lurcher* conducted the operation after a call at 1:00 P.M. by those aboard the *Mainz* to approach their vessel to offload wounded. Commander Tomkinson, in immediate charge of the destroyer, placed his relatively small craft alongside the starboard side of the stricken light cruiser as it began to settle in the water on an even keel. On board the *Mainz*, the situation was one of complete devastation; many of the officers and men had to decide whether to stay at their posts or abandon ship through accepting the British rescue, although by this time many of the crew were leaving the ship of their own accord. Only a portion of the officers and crew were aware of the command to scuttle the ship and probably still fewer were aware that the ship had actually surrendered. The captain of the light cruiser *Southampton* had flashed in International Code the query "Do you surrender?" as the flag of the *Mainz* still flew from the fore-topmast head.[24] The flying flag, however, appears to have been independent of any control on the bridge, which at this point was abandoned amidst the carnage on the ship. Some of the officers and crew, consequently, did not know how to react to the approach of the British. The account of one junior officer, a lieutenant, exhibits the conditions of the rescue and the dilemma.[25] With the decks in ruins, members of the crew continually approached him to ask if they might abandon ship. This officer responded by telling them to remain at their posts while he looked for a more senior officer for guidance. Upon two other lieutenants' coming to his position on the main deck, he asked them what they should do. One of these officers was Lieutenant Wolf Tirpitz, a son of Admiral Alfred von Tirpitz, the creator of the modern German battle fleet. Lieutenant Tirpitz's position had been in the ship's fore-top, and he had remained at his post until the mainmast had slowly collapsed onto the deck. Once it was lying down on deck, Tirpitz had simply walked out of his foretop station. As the *Lurcher* approached, Tirpitz and the other officers suspected that rather than only rescuing the *Mainz's* wounded, the British might board to search for the ship's code books and captain's papers. The original lieutenant consequently passed the order for the crew to get rifles to repel boarders, but most of the weapons the crew produced were either without ammunition or damaged by shell blasts. Instead, the lieutenant decided to oversee the transfer of the wounded to the *Lurcher*. At this point, Commodore Keyes, who oversaw the rescue operation, noticed this lieutenant. Keyes was anxious to cast off from the *Mainz* because the larger cruiser had sunk considerably. If the vessel capsized, the commodore knew it could cause great damage to his ship or render it in danger of sinking also. Keyes tried to bring the young German lieutenant, who was now standing motionless on the poop, aboard. Keyes "shouted to him that he had done splendidly, that there was nothing more he could do, and that he better jump on board quick; and he held out his hand to help him. But the boy scorned to leave his ship as long as she remained afloat, or to accept the slightest favour from his adversary. Drawing himself up stiffly, he slipped back, saluted, and answered: 'Thank you, no.'"[26] Tirpitz also did not choose to go aboard Keyes's flagship. Instead, he went to the bridge amidst the pleas of the paymaster to abandon ship.

Keyes's decision to clear the *Mainz* with some 220 survivors proved a timely one, as at 1:08 P.M. the *Mainz* sank farther down by the head to the point that the propellers, now in the air, nearly smashed into the commodore's flagship. As the *Lurcher* pulled away, the German light cruiser took on a further list to port. Ringed around the vessel were British warships. About this time, the lieutenant who had elected to stay on board heard a great roar from below decks while the *Mainz* began to capsize to port. At 1:10 P.M., the German light cruiser sank by the bow. Both this lieutenant and Tirpitz were taken aboard the light cruiser *Liverpool* for internment in Britain. While British treatment was good, an event early in their capture was surely a source of dismay: "We . . . were kindly received in the wardroom. On the table lay a copy of *Jane's Fighting Ships of the World*—a line had been drawn through the name S.M.S. *Mainz!*"[27] Even so, these same officers were cheered as well by receipt of a telegram from one of the British commanders; his identity is unknown, but rather than being the "admiral" in Tirpitz's account, it was probably Commodore Goodenough. Tirpitz wrote, "Shortly after I came on board the captain sent for me and read me a wireless message from his admiral: 'I am proud to be able to welcome such gallant officers on board my squadron.' I repeated this message to my comrades. It cheered us up, for it showed that the *Mainz* had made an honourable end."[28] The sentiments of the British were true, as numerous accounts speak of the esteem in which British officers and servicemen held the crew of the *Mainz* after their fight.

The sinking of the *Mainz* did not really improve the position of the British force in the bight. By the time that Goodenough ceased fire at 12:25 P.M., Tyrwhitt had resumed his westward sweep with a force that was had been degraded by continuous action. The repairs made to his flagship's feed tank began to fail, and the ship consequently began to once again lose speed. Also, three of his destroyers, *Laurel, Liberty*, and *Laertes*, were damaged. While Tyrwhitt tried to clear the area, eight more German light cruisers were converging on his position. The light cruisers *Stettin* and *Strassburg* remained in proximity to Tyrwhitt while *Köln, Stralsund, München, Danzig*, and *Kolberg* all approached. In addition to these was the light cruiser *Ariadne*. At 12:07 P.M., the captain of this vessel informed Maas in the *Köln* that he was leaving his patrol position off the mouth of the Jade River toward the British position. Further reinforcements were working up for combat following Maas's receipt of a message from the *Mainz*, which proved to be the ship's last. This wireless transmission of 12:03 P.M. indicated that the *Mainz* was under attack by an enemy armored cruiser. Hipper by this time felt he possessed a reasonable amount of information on the composition of the British force. This met Ingenohl's requirement concerning the use of the German battle cruisers in the bight. Unaware of the presence of Beatty's battle cruisers, Hipper at 12:07 P.M. issued orders to the battle cruisers *Moltke* and *Von Der Tann:* "Go to support. Seydlitz follows."[29] Although the *Seydlitz* was not fully operational owing to the trouble with one of its condensers that hindered its speed, Hipper was prepared to commit his force. In addition, the *Blucher* soon received orders to follow the *Seydlitz* when possible. By the time this order was issued, the tide allowed for the passage of these larger ships over the Jade Bar.

In this situation and while the *Mainz* was still in the process of being destroyed, multiple and successive actions began to unfold within a radius of only eight miles. These encounters began when Tyrwhitt at 12:25 P.M. sighted two more light cruisers bearing down on his position from the north. These proved to be Maas in the *Köln* and the *Strassburg*. These two ships had managed to maneuver into proximity of one another and mounted an attack upon sighting the British force. Commodore Keyes was in a poor position at this time because of the damage to his force and the fact that the destroyer flotillas were not reformed in the wake of their numerous engagements. The reduced speed of the *Arethusa* prevented the flagship's participation in the battle. The light cruiser *Fearless*, accompanied by the destroyers *Lizard, Phoenix*, and *Goshawk*, steered toward the Germans to defend Tyrwhitt. The German light cruisers badly out-gunned the British ships. Tyrwhitt considered his situation a dire one. In recounting the battle, Tyrwhitt wrote that as German shells landed around his vessel, "I was really beginning to feel quite blue."[30]

The situation, however, altered entirely at 12:30 P.M. when the hard-pressed British saw large, dark shapes in the mist, which turned out to be Beatty's five battle cruisers. The comment of a British officer on one of Tyrwhitt's destroyers communicates the joy felt by the British at the timely support of these powerful warships: "[T]here straight ahead of us in lovely procession, like elephants walking through a pack of pi-dogs [piss dogs], came our battle cruisers. How solid they looked, how utterly earth-quaking!"[31] Both Maas in the *Köln* and Captain Retzmann of the *Strassburg* certainly agreed with the general appraisal of this officer concerning the power of the ships that bore down on them from the west. The battle cruisers, with armament consisting of 13.5-inch pieces and 12-inch weapons, as well as a variety of smaller caliber guns, far outgunned the two German light cruisers. In addition, the heavy armor of the British ships could resist any shellfire the *Köln* and *Strassburg* could bring to bear. Captain Retzmann's *Strassburg* lay west of *Köln* and was consequently nearer the approaching British. He immediately bore off on a course to the northeast to try an escape. Retzmann succeeded after being in contact with Beatty's battle cruisers a full twelve minutes. The British force passed some 7,200 yards away as the *Strassburg* disappeared into the mist. Maas in the *Köln*, on the other hand, was unable to escape as his response proved less quick than Retzmann's, and the speed of Beatty's force, at the time 27 knots, outmatched the *Köln's* maximum speed.

Maas's ship, as it altered course northeast, was in plain sight of Beatty's approaching battle cruisers. The rear admiral had raced past the four light cruisers of Goodenough's force and seen the burning wreck of the *Mainz*, but he had chosen not to engage. He had clearly seen that the German light cruiser posed no further threat. The next sighting of an enemy ship proved to be the *Köln*, and Beatty gave the order to open fire. The main gun turrets of the *Lion* and the other battle cruisers slowly swung onto target, and at 12:37 P.M. opened fire. The guns of the battle cruisers made short work of Maas's flagship. Within a space of between two and three minutes of the action, the battle cruisers crippled the *Köln* and ensured that it would not escape destruction. Its survival, however, was prolonged when Beatty sighted another German light cruiser at a range of six thousand yards off *Lion's* starboard bow and chose to engage it before the vessel had an opportunity to close within torpedo range.

This vessel was the light cruiser *Ariadne* under the command of Captain Seebohm, who sortied to support Maas. The captain was not entirely aware of the position of the enemy. He had sighted only Lieutenant Commander Ernest Leir's British submarine *E-4*, which had unsuccessfully launched a torpedo attack, off the German coast. Even so, Seebohm steered a course into the bight toward the sound of the guns. The sight of Beatty's battle cruisers completely surprised Seebohm, as no intelligence reports revealed the presence of such large warships at that position in the bight. Maas did not shed light on the situation because the radio room of the *Köln* was wrecked by the battle cruisers' first salvo that had found its mark. Captain Retzmann issued a report that he was being chased by an enemy armored cruiser, but it was received only at 1:00 P.M. due to British jamming. At that same time, Seebohm's vessel came into sight ahead of the British. The German light cruiser had no chance of survival as the captain ordered a course southeast in an effort to escape.

The first British shell hit the *Ariadne* in the forward boiler room, which caused a fire and forced the evacuation of the compartment due to smoke. The ship consequently lost the steam provided by five of its boilers, and the maximum speed of the ship was reduced to 15 knots. Over the course of the next half hour, the British battle cruisers shelled the *Ariadne* at ranges that varied between 6,000 yards and 3,300 yards. Seebohm's vessel endured a multitude of hits, particularly in the stern area of the hull, which became enveloped in a massive fire. The ship also took several hits in the forward section that produced the same type of blaze, but below the main deck. One of the shells that landed in the forward area penetrated the armor deck and destroyed the torpedo room, while another detonated in the sick bay, killing all within it. Curiously, the amidships portion of the vessel remained largely intact. With the ship in this condition, at 1:10 P.M. the Germans observed the British battle cruisers turning away from them. Beatty had decided to disengage for two reasons. The rear admiral possessed reports that destroyers had sighted mines to the east, and he did not want to risk his vessels in a pursuit into the area that supposedly contained the underwater weapons. He also wished to "remain concentrated to meet eventualities."[32] The desire not to disperse British forces too much was based on Beatty's concern that other, larger German warships might be en route to support the German light cruisers. The rear admiral consequently gave the general order to British forces to retire from the bight and altered course to the north to hunt down the *Köln*, which by this time had vanished in the mist.

The withdrawal of Beatty's force did not mean that the *Ariadne* was able to withdraw from the area. The damage inflicted on the ship proved too great for the damage-control parties to repair, and Seebohm could not extinguish the fires that consumed his vessel. The shell hits that penetrated the hull destroyed the fire extinguishing system located on the armor deck just below the main deck. Soon after Beatty's withdrawal, the crew could no longer enter the forward or aft portion of the ship due to the flames. Trapped crewmen also could not escape these areas and died in the fires. These blazes apparently were fueled by the paint that covered the hull. According to one German sailor, the paint was one-quarter-inch thick due to repeated applications.[33] The fact that the engine room, aft boiler room, and steering gear remained intact and allowed for the ship to retreat from the area was little comfort to the captain. Seebohm fully appreciated the immediate danger that the fires might detonate the magazines, destroy the ship, and kill a large portion of the crew. Indeed, ready ammunition by the guns began to explode and spray splinters through the air. While Seebohm was able to establish that the forward magazine was flooded, he was not able to reach the aft magazine and check its condition. Therefore, the captain decided, amidst the intense fire, heat, and finally the smoke that wreathed his vessel, to issue the order to abandon ship. The crew collected what wounded they could and joined the captain on the forecastle, where Seebohm called for three hurrahs for Kaiser Wilhelm II, and the crew, including the wounded, then sang "Deutschland, Deutschland, Über Alles." Around 2:00 P.M., the light cruiser *Danzig* arrived to help evacuate the ship.

While events unfolded with the *Ariadne*, the other German light cruisers arrived piecemeal on the scene of the action. All bore off as each either faced superior numbers or received information of the British force strength in the bight. At 1:06 P.M., the *Stralsund* approached Beatty from the south and encountered the three light cruisers that remained with Goodenough (the *Liverpool* had stayed with the *Mainz* to rescue survivors, while the *Nottingham* and the *Lowestoft* remained lost as a result of the weather). This light cruiser would have arrived sooner, as it had left Wilhelmshaven at 10:00 A.M., but the ship's Captain Harder steered a course around what had been identified as a field of mines, and thus he lengthened his transit time to the battle zone. In actuality, the "minefield" comprised floating, spent shell cartridges from earlier combat. Nevertheless, Harder altered his course northeast to parallel Goodenough's light cruisers and subsequently opened fire. With continued low visibility in the bight, the German gun crews could not see the fall of their shot in order to correct their aim, but even so the *Stralsund*'s fire proved accurate from the opening of the engagement. The German vessel's first salvo landed only fifty yards astern of the *Southampton*. The British return fire, however, cut the wireless transmission aerial wires of Harder's ship, and another shell hit the hull beneath the waterline, but failed to explode. These hits led Harder to haul away in the face of a superior force and retreat southeast. Harder steamed in this direction until 1:30 P.M., when he hoped that he was clear of the British. Goodenough chose not to pursue, in keeping with the order from Beatty to retire from the bight.

Fog generally saved from destruction the other light cruisers that were in the immediate area in the minutes approaching 1:00 P.M. that afternoon. The light cruiser *Stettin* briefly reacquired the British at 12:40 P.M., when German lookouts aboard it sighted the *Ariadne*, but after being engaged briefly by the 12-inch guns of the battle cruiser *New Zealand*, Captain Nerger decided to retreat east. Soon thereafter, Nerger encountered the light cruiser *Danzig* under the command of Captain Reiss. After Nerger warned Reiss of the presence of enemy battle cruisers, both retired east. Captain Retzmann in the *Strassburg* encountered at 1:30 P.M. Beatty's battle cruisers on a course northeast at a range of eight thousand yards. Retzmann used the fog in the bight to pass his four-funneled ship off as one of the *Town*-class light cruisers of Goodenough's force. As he sped from the area, at 1:35 , the *Strassburg* became the first German vessel of the day to clearly communicate to the high command that German forces in the bight faced battle cruisers.[34] This information prompted commander in chief of the High Seas Fleet Admiral Ingenohl minutes later to recall all light cruisers in the bight.

This order could not save the *Köln* from destruction. Indeed, Retzmann owed his escape in part to the fact that Beatty had reacquired the flagship of Rear Admiral Leberecht Maas and was intent on finishing off the work of the earlier engagement. At 1:25 P.M. with a range of only four thousand yards, Beatty opened fire on Maas's crippled vessel. Despite his hopeless situation, Maas proved game for battle. The light cruiser *Köln* fired some two hundred rounds and hit the *Lion* five times. To the British aboard Beatty's flagship, it appeared that Maas was directing his fire on the conning tower of the British ship to try to disable it through a damaging hit to the control center. This effort proved entirely ineffective due to the heavy armor protection of the conning tower. Captain Chatfield related that "[o]ne felt the tiny four-inch shell spatter against the conning tower armour, and the pieces 'sizz' over it."[35] The only damage caused to the *Lion* came from a hit at the base of B turret. While the small shell did not penetrate through the giant turret's armor, the explosion did destroy some electrical wiring inside it. Nevertheless, this did not impede the ship's fighting ability.

On the other hand, the damage wrought by the heavy guns of the British devastated the *Köln* in short order. The only account of the terrible ordeal that unfolded was written by the sole survivor of the *Köln*, stoker Adolf Neumann. Among the first hits was one that destroyed the conning tower, killing Maas and all others within it. Additional hits knocked out the engine rooms and boilers, destroyed the ship's steering gear, and tore out one side of the hull. Neumann, describing the last minutes of his ship, wrote:

> [A]lmost every gun had received a direct hit. Many of them had been hurled from their mountings; the armored shields were pierced and torn. Mutilated bodies lay in heaps amidst a jumble of smashed boats, davits, iron ladders, spars, wireless antennae, ammunition, and shell fragments. The bridge had vanished; each of the three funnels were riddled through and through; shell holes of enormous diameter appeared in the superstructure. Officers and men, including a number of wounded, assembled at the stern. . . . The ship still floated on an even keel, but she was sinking rapidly.[36]

Amidst the destruction and the word to abandon ship, some 250 men gathered on the quarterdeck, where they gave three hurrahs and sang the "Flag

Song." They also said goodbye to the chief engineer, who stayed aboard in order to plant scuttling charges in the hull of the *Köln* to speed the vessel's sinking. Neumann, after he abandoned ship and while he floated in the water holding onto two life jackets, witnessed from a distance of one hundred meters the end of the *Köln*: "[A] white smoke-cloud shot high out of the forecastle and then another from the poop, no explosion. First the bow came out of the water; then, following the white smoke cloud from the poop, the stern with rudder and propellers; then the ship listed over to port and sank."[37] The *Köln* broke in half, thanks in large part to the scuttling charges, at 1:35 P.M. and sank. The action had taken only about ten minutes.

Beatty's last action proved to be a humanitarian one, as he endeavored to rescue the survivors in the water. Tragically, the British picked up none of the estimated 250 men who survived the sinking of the *Köln*, as according to one British naval officer a submarine was sighted. Beatty did not want to risk any of his force in the face of an underwater craft, and so the British felt forced to "leave a few poor devils to their fate."[38] In fact, there were no submarines in the area. All the survivors but Neumann later succumbed to the rough conditions of the North Sea. German torpedo boats picked him out of the water on 30 August, after over seventy hours of exposure to the elements.

The destruction of the *Köln* proved to be the last engagement of the Battle of Heligoland Bight. Beatty now shaped a course out of the area. By 1:50 P.M., all British units were out of the combat area of the bight and en route to Britain. They would not be pursued by units of the German fleet, in part because of the general order for the light cruisers to retire. Also, however, Ingenohl prevented any units of the High Seas Fleet from steaming into the bight despite the fact that by 1:35 P.M. Battle Squadrons I and III of the High Seas Fleet were raising steam to sortie into the bight if necessary, and Hipper's battle cruisers were already in the process of steaming into the bight. Upon receiving the *Strassburg's* message that reported the presence of Beatty's battle cruisers, the commander in chief of the High Seas Fleet acted in the way dictated by his operational orders. According to his standing orders, the battle fleet would engage the enemy only under favorable conditions. While Ingenohl was not aware of any German ships being sunk at this point, he did believe that the situation in the bight did not appear to match the stipulation of the operational order. Also, any loss of large surface vessels would defeat the intention of whittling down the numerical strength of the British navy in preparation for a decisive battle. Ingenohl, consequently, issued an order to Hipper that "[b]attle cruisers are not to engage the battle cruiser squadron."[39] The subsequent movements of the German Navy on 28 August were governed by the utmost caution to prevent further loss. By the time the High Seas Fleet arrived in force into the bight, the British had already left the area. The Battle of Heligoland Bight, the first pitched naval engagement of World War I, was over.

CHAPTER FIVE

THE AFTERMATH OF THE BATTLE AND ITS RAMIFICATIONS ON THE WAR AT SEA

I N THE IMMEDIATE AFTERMATH of the battle, as British forces steamed out of the bight, German forces still in the area, the light cruisers, endeavored to make contact with one another while heavier units of the High Seas Fleet began to sortie into the area to make sense of the situation. By the time of the British withdrawal, the Germans, owing to their communication problems and the confusing nature of the battle, were not yet completely aware of the losses the fleet had suffered that day or all of the specifics of the battle itself.

While the heavy units of the High Seas Fleet still lay outside the battle zone, around 1:50 P.M. the light cruiser *Danzig* lay near the stricken *Ariadne* if needed to offload survivors from Captain Seebohm's vessel. Minutes later, the *Stralsund* and the *Kolberg* arrived on the scene to aid in the operation (the *Strassburg* came up some time later). The *Kolberg*, under the command of Captain Widenmann, had arrived too late to participate in the battle, but assumed a position northwest of the other two cruisers to patrol in order to warn of any approach by British vessels that may still be in the area. When just before 3:00 P.M. Seebohm gave the order to abandon ship, the *Danzig* came close and offloaded the crew, which had gathered on the forecastle while Seebohm and his officers remained on the bridge. By the time the *Danzig* completed its task, the captain of the *Ariadne* saw that the fires on his vessel had largely burned themselves out and believed his ship could be brought safely back to port under tow. He consequently took a boat over to the *Stralsund* and asked its Captain Harder to take the *Ariadne* in tow, but this plan proved stillborn. At 3:25 P.M. the light cruiser *Ariadne* heeled over to port before finally capsizing to starboard, as the result apparently of a boiler explosion that further damaged the hull. The upturned ship remained afloat for some time afterward.

The heavier units of the High Seas Fleet arrived in time to view the *Ariadne's* last moments. At 2:45 P.M., the battle cruisers *Moltke* and *Von Der Tann* arrived on the scene under the command of Rear Admiral Tapken. The delay in the arrival of these units was the result of the very cautious, slow advance they had made into the bight. The order issued by Ingenohl that forbade them to engage enemy battle cruisers was in part to blame for this situation. In addition, Tapken knew very little about the overall situation. No German vessel had received a report from the *Mainz* or the *Köln* in about two hours, and Hipper, Tapken's superior, did not even know of the number of battle cruisers reported in the bight. Before this time, all reports on enemy battle cruisers had gone to Ingenohl, and he had not informed Hipper of the British force composition of battle cruisers.[1] Hipper consequently further slowed down his ship's arrival on the scene. He ordered Tapken to wait for the arrival of the *Seydlitz*, Hipper's flagship, before entering the bight. The flagship, however, was slow due to the trouble with its port condenser that reduced the vessel's maximum speed. Also, Hipper was slower in arriving as he waited for the armored cruiser *Blucher* to make ready for sea before leaving Wilhelmshaven. Hipper consequently arrived at the *Ariadne's* position at 3:10 P.M. behind Tapken, while the armored cruiser *Blucher* lay farther behind and did not reached the area for another fifty minutes after Hipper's arrival. Like the officers and crew of the other two battle cruisers, Hipper and his men therefore witnessed the sinking of the *Ariadne* before the commander of the scouting forces took steps to secure the bight. Hipper ordered the light cruisers *Stralsund*, *Strassburg*, and *Kolberg* to proceed north-northwest on a reconnaissance sweep with the three battle cruisers following in support. Accompanying them also were the craft of Torpedo Boat Flotilla VIII, which had arrived on the scene in keeping with Hipper's order to patrol the inner bight for submarines. These torpedo boats formed a defensive screen around the larger vessels.

By now, Hipper was convinced that the *Mainz* and the *Köln* were sunk despite his not having yet received any definitive report on the matter. His primary concern now lay in making sure that no British forces remained in the area and reestablishing the defense of the bight. The reconnaissance sweep revealed no British warships, but it was of only a limited nature because of the order not to engage enemy battle cruisers. The cautious nature of this advance proved to have a terrible consequence, as one of the light cruisers approached as close as four miles to the spot where the survivors of the *Köln* floated in the water before turning around. This tragic circumstance led to only stoker Neumann surviving the sinking of the ship. This ineffective reconnaissance sweep took place amidst some confusion as Ingenohl anxiously wired Hipper about the situation in the bight and whether more large warships were needed there. As late as 3:45 P.M., Ingenohl ordered the battleships in Squadron I of the High Seas Fleet to anchor at Schillig Roads as soon as possible in preparation for possible action, while at 4:24 P.M. Hipper received the message "CSF (Commander Scouting Forces) report immediately whether support by battleships is necessary. Comdr (sic) High Seas."[2] Eleven minutes later Ingenohl received Hipper's response that he had sighted no British warships and was already on a course with his battle cruisers and the armored cruiser *Blucher* back to the Jade River. Hipper had decided on this action by 4:00 P.M. in order to make port by nightfall.

While Hipper made his way back to Wilhelmshaven, the reestablishment of the defense of the bight was under way. At 3:31 P.M. Hipper signaled all units of Torpedo Boat Flotillas I and V, the much-abused craft attacked during the day, to steam from Heligoland back to Wilhelmshaven. The ten ships of Torpedo Boat Flotilla VIII took up positions on the outer defense line of the bight patrol, while minesweepers again gained the inner patrol line. The light cruisers *Kolberg*, *München*, and *Hela* took positions as the support craft for the night. By sunset, the bight patrol was back in place as Hipper continued to make his way back to Wilhelmshaven. Along the way, the commander of scouting forces garnered more information on the exact force strength of the enemy over the course of the past day and began to brief Ingenohl. Only at 6:17 P.M. did Ingenohl finally receive a more complete picture of the forces that had faced the German patrols that day: "Taking part in the engagement were several Town class cruisers, several single armored cruisers of Shannon type, four battle cruisers, Lion type . . ."[3] Even this report was not accurate and indicates the confused nature of the battle for the Germans. No *Shannon*-class vessels participated in the contest, and Beatty actually had five battle cruisers. Only two of these were *Lion*-class, although the *Queen Mary* was a very similar ship to the other two, while the other vessels bore no resemblance in terms of their silhouettes. Indeed, German intelligence was such that the high command could not absolutely confirm the loss of the *Mainz* and the *Köln* until the British press reported their sinking and provided a complete picture of events from the British point of view.[4] Equipped with rather spotty information, Hipper dropped anchor off Wilhelmshaven at 8:03 P.M. that night. He immediately made his way to the battleship *Friedrich Der Grosse*, Ingenohl's flagship, to make a full report. His wireless message from 6:17 P.M., despite its inaccuracy, as well as the myriad reports received over the course of the battle that indicated a large number of destroyers, formed the beginning of the German appraisal of the engagement. On a wider scale, the meeting between Hipper and Ingenohl represents the beginning of the German reaction to the Battle of Heligoland Bight and its impact on the war at sea in World War I.

As the Germans took stock of their situation and reconstituted their defense of Heligoland Bight, the British were proceeding as quickly as possible out of the area. All British forces had cleared the bight by 1:50 P.M., and given the damage to the light cruiser *Arethusa* along with the three destroyers as well as the threat of further, much heavier German resistance, Tyrwhitt, Keyes, and Beatty certainly wanted to expedite the endeavor. The threat of large warships such as battle cruisers or even light cruisers was not the only one. At 2:50 P.M., *S-165* of Torpedo Boat Flotilla III located at the Ems River reported sighting two enemy destroyers and a light cruiser on a southwest course some 35 miles north of Borkum, but the craft was ordered to withdraw due to lack of light cruiser support.[5] In addition, the British feared submarine attack. Both the battle cruiser *Queen Mary* and the light cruiser *Lowestoft* reported attacks by enemy submarines on the voyage home.[6] Both of these sightings proved false, as the Germans had no submarines in the area at the time. Nevertheless, they reinforced the British commanders' decision to remove their forces from the area as quickly as possible.

The condition of the damaged vessels in the British force hampered this effort. Tyrwhitt's flagship as well as the destroyer *Laurel* could make only 10 knots because of their condition. The task force thus limped home at this speed. The severe damage to the *Laertes* led the destroyer *Lapwing* to take the ship in tow for some minutes, but the tow line broke. Captain Blunt in the *Fearless* subsequently took over this task. Blunt, accompanied by these damaged craft and the Fifth Division, First Flotilla, steamed some eight miles to the east of the other twenty-three destroyers in the British force, which formed a defensive ring around Tyrwhitt's ship. Nearby also were Beatty's battle cruisers and Goodenough's light cruisers, including the *Nottingham* and the *Lowestoft*. At 2:30 P.M., these two ships, after having been lost to the rest of the force for most of the engagement, had managed to join back up with the rest of the First Light Cruiser Squadron. All of Goodenough's light cruisers remained with Beatty with the exception of the *Liverpool*, which Beatty detached at 7:45 P.M. to transport the eighty-six officers and men that the cruiser took aboard from the *Mainz* to Rosyth. Among them was Lieutenant Wolf Tirpitz.

By the time that the *Liverpool* left the force, the old armored cruisers of Rear Admiral Christian had further augmented the British force. In the late afternoon, these ships had come up to Tyrwhitt. Beatty had ordered this force to proceed as support toward the battered ships of the raid as they made their withdrawal. The sight of these ships certainly was a welcome one. Christian first encountered Commodore Keyes in the *Lurcher* at 4:30 P.M. and easily saw the mass of survivors from the *Mainz* that crowded the forecastle of the destroyer. The rear admiral subsequently transferred 165 unwounded Germans of a total of 224 to the armored cruiser *Cressy* and ordered it and the *Bacchante* to make a course for the Nore.[7] Despite Keyes's comments about these old ships, the commodore was certainly happy for this service. The commodore had shipped 224 prisoners on his vessel while the destroyer was manned by only 70 officers and men. Of these Keyes required 20 of them in the ship's machinery spaces, leaving only 50 to watch over the Germans.[8] Christian also came upon the crippled destroyer *Laurel* and used the light cruiser *Amethyst* to tow the vessel the rest of the way back to Britain. Christian's final service was to Tyrwhitt in the *Arethusa* as by 7:00 P.M. the maximum speed of the flagship of the Harwich Force had dropped to 6 knots. So low was this speed, due to the ship's steadily failing machinery, that Beatty had ordered Tyrwhitt to draw the fires in his boilers to await the arrival of Christian's armored cruisers. The light cruiser *Arethusa* had glided to a stop, dead in the water. Captain Wilmot Nicholson of the armored cruiser *Hogue*, another of Christian's force, relieved this situation. Nicholson, a friend of Tyrwhitt's, approached the *Arethusa*, established contact with the query "Is that you, Reggie?" and then took the flagship of the Harwich Force in tow. Tyrwhitt later wrote that "I never was so glad to see him before."[9] The other armored cruisers of Christian's force—*Euryalus*, his flagship, and *Aboukir*—took ten undamaged destroyers of the Harwich Force and reestablished a patrol at Terschelling that had been a task of Cruiser Force C since the beginning of the war.

The remainder of the British force continued on its slow journey back to Britain. On 29 August Beatty, who now felt assured that all vessels were out of danger, shaped a course northward with Goodenough's ships back to Scapa Flow. The ships of Beatty's First Battle Cruiser Squadron ultimately did not anchor at their base until the following day because Beatty received orders to conduct a further operation. By that time, all of the rest of the force was safely in port. The armored cruiser *Hogue* towed the *Arethusa* to Chatham dockyard for repairs, accompanied by a few undamaged destroyers as well as the damaged ones, the latter also in need of repair at the yard. The rest of the Harwich Force as well as Keyes's vessels returned to Harwich, while Rear Admiral Moore's battle cruisers, *Invincible* and *New Zealand*, anchored in the Firth of Forth.

By the time that the first ships arrived in port, the celebration amongst the British populace was already under way due to press releases by the Admiralty on the battle. Even before Tyrwhitt's vessel dropped anchor at Chatham, British civilians sighted his battered vessel being towed by the *Hogue* and cheered what they considered a British naval victory over Germany. These people, however, came to a mistaken conclusion concerning Tyrwhitt's flagship:

> [T]he two ships . . . were overtaken by a crowded Margate steamer, which passed them quite close and whose passengers evidently concluded that the British cruiser was bringing in a captured German prize. While overtaking the *Arethusa* they stared in silence and some awe at her holed and battered side, but when they came abreast of the *Hogue* they broke into enthusiastic cheering and yelling which they kept up until they were out of hearing.[10]

The action of the crowd prompted Tyrwhitt to signal to his friend that he suspected they thought the *Hogue* was bringing in a captured German warship as a
prize. Nicholson responded that in a sense he did indeed have a prize: "And so
I have, but not the sort they think."[11] These words proved quite apt, as Nicholson
paid tribute to the role of the *Arethusa* in the battle. Aside from the people on
the Margate steamer, so did the British populace pay tribute to their navy. As the
Arethusa neared Sheerness on its way to Chatham, Tyrwhitt was met by throngs
of cheering people who already knew of the British victory in Heligoland Bight.
Among the masses waiting for Tyrwhitt at Sheerness was First Lord Churchill,
who excitedly boarded the flagship and, in Tyrwhitt's words, "fairly slobbered"
over him. Churchill called on Tyrwhitt to give him a blow-by-blow account of
the battle and promised him any ship that he desired while the *Arethusa* under-
went repairs. Overnight, Tyrwhitt had become a British naval hero.

The same reception met other units of the raiding force. Goodenough's light
cruisers arrived at Scapa Flow at 8:00 P.M. on 29 August on what proved to be a
fine summer's evening. As the light cruisers passed the battleships of the Grand
Fleet, sailors aboard them gave cheers to the men of the First Light Cruiser
Squadron. Crewmembers of the battleship *Orion* even went so far as to help the
men of the light cruiser *Southampton* re-coal their ship once it dropped anchor. This service was a truly great one, as the process of coaling a ship was a
very laborious and dirty job in which coal dust coated all surfaces of the vessel
and the men involved in the task. Indeed, one officer aboard the *Southampton*
asserted that he never saw such a favor bestowed again by any crew to another.[12]
Beatty received a similar reception, although his return did not prove quite as
smooth as Goodenough's. When Beatty steamed into Scapa Flow on 30 August
to the same cheers as those given to the First Light Cruiser Squadron, the *Lion*
had to make two approaches to its moorings due to suffering a fouled anchor
chain on the first attempt. This annoyed Beatty, as he thought the second pass
might be misinterpreted by some as being a haughty gesture. His fears, however, were put to rest by another admiral in the port, who signaled, "It seems
your anchor was rammed home as hard as your attack."[13] The admiral's comment was meant as a compliment as much as reassurance. Indeed, Beatty's reputation enjoyed the greatest increase both in the navy and in the British press.

The losses inflicted on the Germans by Beatty as well as the other commanders did on the surface justify the enthusiasm of the men in the British navy as
well as the civilian population. The German forces involved in the defense of
Heligoland Bight suffered heavily with very little to show for it. In terms of material, Germany lost three light cruisers, the *Mainz*, the *Köln*, and the *Ariadne*,
along with torpedo boat *V-187*, while destroying none of the attacking force.
While the loss of *V-187* was relatively minor, that of the three light cruisers was
not, as Germany did not have many craft of their type. At the start of the war,
Germany operated only sixteen such vessels.[14] The Germans needed light

cruisers to perform the task of scouting for the battle fleet, a primary mission of such ships, as well as for defense of the bight. For a time, until more light cruisers came into service, the loss of a quarter of their force certainly hampered future operations. The first two new cruisers were not completed until December 1914 and January 1915, while others would not be complete until mid-1915. More devastating than the loss of ships, however, was the human toll.[15] The Germans suffered 712 officers and men killed, with an additional 158 wounded. The capture of 381 more officers and men further added to the total of individuals taken from the ranks of the German navy. Of the total of 1,251 officers and men killed, wounded, and captured, the majority came from the light cruisers *Köln* and *Mainz*. The destruction of the former ship resulted in the death of Rear Admiral Leberecht Maas, the first German loss of an admiral in World War I. His death alone was significant, as it deprived Germany of one of its best commanders as well as one of the most aggressive. All but one of *Köln's* crew died either during the battle, in the sinking, or from exposure to the elements once they abandoned ship. The total stood at 489 officers and men. The German navy lost 437 of the crew of the light cruiser *Mainz*: 89 of these were dead officers and men, while the other 348 people were those captured during the British rescue operation. The light cruiser *Ariadne's* crew suffered the deaths of 3 officers and 61 crewmen. The sinking of torpedo boat V-187 accounted for 24 officers and crew dead and a further 30 captured men. The rest of the German total resulted from casualties aboard torpedo boat V-1 of Torpedo Boat Flotilla V and minesweepers D-8 and T-33 of the inner patrol line in the bight defense. The deaths of all of these men weighed heavily on the minds of all those in the navy as well as the kaiser himself.

In return, the British suffered relatively little material or human loss for their raid. No British ship sank, despite there being heavy damage to the light cruiser *Arethusa* as well as the destroyers *Laurel*, *Liberty*, and *Laertes*. The damage to Tyrwhitt's flagship led to its immediately being taken out of service once it docked at Chatham. Repairs took a little under three weeks. This comparatively light damage to the British raiding force produced few casualties: 35 officers and men killed and 40 wounded. The *Arethusa* suffered the greatest loss, with 11 killed and 16 wounded, which is actually rather slight in comparison to the damage taken by the ship. The destroyer *Laurel* suffered almost as many casualties, with the death of 11 officers and men and the wounding of 11 others.

The greatest impact of the Battle of Heligoland Bight in Britain was a product of the lopsided material losses of the Germans versus those of the British. The victory was a great morale boost to the British populace at a time when it was sorely needed, given that the German Army was driving into France. Indeed, according to Commodore Keyes it also proved a great comfort to the troops of the Entente powers that struggled to stop the German advance: "We were told the news of our naval success, which was circulated to the Allied

Armies, greatly heartened our weary, hard-pressed troops."[16] It also ended the initial period of frustration felt by the British populace over the inaction at the beginning of the war. Britain's major newspapers trumpeted the battle as a great triumph for the country. Among these was a *Daily Express* headline that read "We've Gone to Heligoland and Back. Please God, We'll Go Again!" Between 29 August and 31 August, the *Times* of London echoed the sentiments of the *Daily Express*, although the titles of their pieces did not smack of the same headiness as the *Express's*. The first British articles of 29 August read "Victory for the Fleet" and "A Brilliant Action," while a follow-up article labeled the battle a "Bolt from the Blue."[17] The feeling of the people is certainly evident from the reception that Tyrwhitt received on the way to Chatham. The same can be said of the reaction among British sailors, as they cheered Goodenough's light cruisers and Beatty's battle cruisers on their arrival back in port.

The sense of triumph felt by the British people and regular sailors, however, was not felt as greatly among the administration and officers of the Royal Navy. Perhaps the greatest source of enthusiasm in the Admiralty over the outcome of the raid was first lord of the Admiralty Winston Churchill. Not only had he been present to receive Tyrwhitt as he arrived back in Britain, but Churchill later labeled the action a "brilliant episode" and wrote that "British light forces were rampaging about the enemy's most intimate and jealously guarded waters."[18] Churchill, however, did acknowledge that the operation suffered greatly as a result of the lack of coordination in the Admiralty from the start of the endeavor. Churchill summed up the situation where Goodenough's and Beatty's ships were exposed to the danger of submarine attack from a lack of intelligence information: "Several awkward embarrassments followed from this and might easily have led to disastrous mistakes."[19] Even so, the first lord chose in later years to emphasize the material loss of the enemy and took special note of the impact he believed the battle had on German morale. In his book *The World Crisis*, Churchill asserted that

> [m]uch more important . . . was the effect produced on the morale of the enemy. The Germans knew nothing of our defective staff work or the risks we had run. All they saw was that the British did not hesitate to hazard their greatest vessels as well as their light craft in the most daring offensive action and had escaped apparently unscathed. They felt as we should have felt had German destroyers broken into the Solent and their battle-cruisers had penetrated as far as the Nab.[20]

While this analysis is true to an extent, it was not one universally accepted by other members of the Admiralty or the naval officers involved the effort.

On the whole, the Admiralty and British naval officer corps reacted disparagingly when they analyzed the outcome of the battle. Many focused on the general lack of coordination in the Admiralty as the dominant problem that greatly detracted from the usefulness of the raid. This had hampered the movements of naval forces in the battle. They also believed that this same problem had presented the possibility of the battle resulting in disaster from friendly vessels being mistaken for the enemy and destroyed. The reaction of assistant director of operations, Naval Staff Captain Herbert Richmond is indicative of that in the naval establishment. On 29 August, Richmond acknowledged the news of the raid into Heligoland Bight and the losses inflicted on the enemy. At first, Richmond felt vindicated by the action, as he had been among the planners of an earlier raid envisioned by Churchill that the Naval Staff had shelved: "I cannot help feeling rather an 'I-told-you-so' feeling. . . . It ought never to have been in doubt that this was the proper move."[21] While the assistant director of operations surely maintained this stance on the matter, his overall assessment of the operation, of which he wrote on 30 August, was certainly not positive. Richmond recorded:

> Anything worse worded than the order for the operation of last Friday [28 August] I have never seen. A mass of latitudes & longitudes, no expression to shew the object of the sweep. . . . Besides the hasty manner in which, all unknown to our submarines, the 1st Light Cruiser Squadron suddenly turned up in a wholly unexpected direction, thereby running the gravest dangers from our own submarines. The weather was fairly foggy, ships came up to one another unexpectedly, & with such omissions & errors in the plan it was truly fortunate that we had no accidents.[22]

The references to the planning indicted Keyes and Tyrwhitt in part as the architects of the plan, but Richmond's comments also implicated the administration of the Naval Staff and the Admiralty in general. Richmond was an outspoken critic of the lack of organization in the Naval Staff, and his criticism carried weight. The orders were not very intricate, and the operation was hastily put together and executed. More important, the lack of information provided by the Admiralty to Tyrwhitt or Keyes about Goodenough's and Beatty's supporting craft nearly did result in disaster.

Many of the officers involved echoed Captain Richmond's sentiments in some form and were quite critical of the entire operation as a result. Chief among them was Commodore Keyes, the architect of the raid into the bight. In a letter of 5 September 1914, to Commodore Goodenough, Keyes wrote that he thought

> an absurd fuss was made over the entire affair, except in regard to the gallant conduct of *Arethusa* and *Fearless* who were continually engaged at intervals for over 5 hours with cruisers superior in number and power. . . . It makes me sick and disgusted to think what a complete success it might have been but for, I won't say dual, but—multiple control. We begged for light cruisers to support us and deal with the Enemy's light cruisers which we knew would

come out. Destroyer's short range guns are no match for light cruiser's guns—but were told that none were available. If you [Goodenough] had only known what we were aiming at, had had an opportunity of discussing it with Tyrwhitt and me, and had been inshore with *Fearless* and *Arethusa* we might have sunk at least six cruisers, and had a "scoop" indeed—(To use the Admiralty word).[23]

Such remarks are not those of an officer who viewed the Battle of Heligoland Bight as a success. In Keyes's mind, it was an operation of very limited gain that failed in its purpose of inflicting great loss on the enemy. The blame, in his mind, rested solely at the feet of the Admiralty. He extended this belief past its application to the surface forces to his own submarines.

Goodenough, for his part, echoed Keyes's lamentation in his response to the 5 September letter. The commodore of the First Light Cruiser Squadron wrote, "I quite agree with all you say about the *Arethusa*. I gnash my teeth when I think I might have saved him half his losses if I hadn't been deflected. I wrote with some strength to Freddie H about it."[24] The term "deflected" refers to the confusion created by the lack of information from the Admiralty to Keyes or Tyrwhitt that Goodenough would be in the area. Goodenough's passages also refer to a letter he wrote to second sea lord of the Admiralty Vice Admiral Sir Frederick Hamilton in which he held poor planning responsible for the near destruction of the light cruiser *Southampton* and submarine *E-4* of Keyes's force. In his memoir, Goodenough later wrote of the lack of coordination and the risk of friendly ships attacking each other and stated that "[s]ome instinct saved us from that. These things happen."[25] This cavalier appraisal did not, however, indicate the commodore's stance on the matter in the wake of the event.

The only officer involved in the action who viewed the outcome of the battle in slightly more favorable terms was Beatty, as he was responsible for the destruction of the light cruisers *Köln* and *Ariadne*, but even he qualified his words. The vice admiral wrote his wife after the battle that the Germans had "fought their ships like men and went down with colours flying like seamen, against overwhelming odds. . . . [I]t was good work to be able to do it within 20 miles of their main base, Heligoland, and with the whole of the High Seas Fleet listening to the boom of our guns."[26] In a subsequent letter, however, Beatty believed that the battle had very nearly been a tragedy for the British navy. On September 2, he wrote that "I had thought I should have received an expression of their appreciation from Their Lordships, but have been disappointed, or rather not so much disappointed as disgusted, and my real opinion has been confirmed that they would have hung me if there had been a disaster, as there nearly was, owing to the extraordinary neglect of the most ordinary precautions on their part. . . . Don't breathe a word of this to a soul, but it's on record."[27] The opinion to which he referred is the one he held on the bridge of the *Lion* during the battle as he struggled with the decision to commit his battle cruisers to the contest. At that time, he feared the loss of one of his ships and the impact such an event would have on his fortunes. One consideration in his mind had been potential torpedo attack by British submarines, although he had discounted it as part of his decision to participate in the engagement. Clearly, Beatty as well recognized the inadequate nature of planning that hampered the operation.

Beatty's letter to his wife also reveals the Admiralty's reaction to the battle overall, which was in keeping with the 30 August appraisal of Captain Richmond. Despite the fact that the Naval War Staff, particularly Chief of Staff Doveton Sturdee, was responsible for the problem that was roundly attacked by all those involved, Keyes, Tyrwhitt, and Goodenough all came under attack from the Admiralty while the nation celebrated the Battle of Heligoland Bight. The naval administration held the commanders of the operation responsible for the confusing nature of the battle and by extension the relatively low losses inflicted on the enemy.[28] While it is true that there was no concrete method of sending orders by wireless over the distance of the bight, the majority of the fault definitely lay with the Admiralty. The hasty dispatch of Beatty and Goodenough with no prior notice meant that the British had to deal with four separate commands: those of Tyrwhitt, Keyes, Beatty, and Goodenough. In addition, for the lion's share of the engagement, thanks to the Admiralty, Keyes did not even know of the presence of the latter two commanders and their respective forces.

Commander in chief of the Grand Fleet Admiral John Jellicoe fully appreciated not only the problems suffered at Heligoland Bight, but also the need for reform to protect against a repeat of the same situation. Jellicoe rendered two conclusions after reading the after-action report of the operation. He believed that there should be far greater coordination between commanders at the tactical level and between the Admiralty and naval commanders. In terms of the former, he noted as evidence the fact that many messages were sent during the battle without vital information such as the course and speed of the enemy or the position of the British vessel sending a message. This criticism focused on Keyes, Tyrwhitt, and Goodenough. Respecting the latter relationship, Jellicoe's call sprang from the poor conditions under which he had hastily sent out Goodenough and Beatty for the operation, which had so hampered it. Jellicoe wrote in terms of cooperation between his Grand Fleet to the north of Britain and those squadrons anchored in southern ports that it "was essential that in any future combined operations full information should be given to all officers commanding units of southern forces as to the ships which are taking part in these operations."[29] Not only did the Admiralty agree with Jellicoe's proposals, but it also took some steps to better communicate which units would take part in battles. Nevertheless, the Naval Staff's penchant for providing little or no information in some cases persisted well after the Battle of Heligoland Bight.

All told, the professional estimation of the Battle of Heligoland Bight amongst British officers and those within the Admiralty was that the battle had produced little real gain and could have resulted in a British disaster rather than a victory. The lack of coordination for the operation was certainly a dominant factor, and fog made the battle all the more confusing. Beyond the threat of British vessels mistaking friendly warships for the enemy and destroying them, these factors certainly did rob the British of some measure of effectiveness in their raid. During the battle, Keyes and Tyrwhitt pursued supposedly enemy ships through the fog that were in actuality those of Goodenough, thus diverting their attention away from the offensive sweep. It also distracted Goodenough from his supporting role. Aside from lack of coordination and the weather, however, several other considerations must be taken into account to explain why the British were exceedingly fortunate and ultimately why the battle unfolded as it did. Indeed, had it not been for the presence of the very light cruisers and battle cruisers that remained largely unknown to Keyes, Tyrwhitt's forces might have been overwhelmed by the German light cruisers that arrived on the scene.

The British effort was also hampered in part by the force composition for the raid, the gunnery and torpedo skills of the sailors who manned the British ships, and the quality of British shells. In terms of the first consideration, the light cruiser *Arethusa* proved largely ineffective in the contest. The ship was brand new and as such was not prepared fully for combat. While two of the vessel's guns jammed in the initial duel with the *Frauenlob*, the German light cruiser, despite being thirteen years older than the British ship and armed only with 4.1-inch guns versus the *Arethusa's* collection of 6-inch and 4-inch pieces, inflicted damage on Tyrwhitt's flagship that left it more of a liability for the remainder of the contest than a factor in it. Had it not been for the one 6-inch gun that scored several hits on the German vessel, the damage to the *Frauenlob* would have been still less than the negligible amount actually inflicted by Tyrwhitt's ship. A second problem was the quality of gunnery and torpedo attacks. While it is true that fog certainly played a role in this problem, by the end of the battle the British had succeeded in sinking only three light cruisers and a destroyer after expending a great deal of ammunition. German officers' accounts repeatedly made light of the British warships' heavy firing with little gain. In addition, for all of the torpedoes launched in the engagement, the British claimed only one hit on the light cruiser *Mainz*. The Admiralty certainly took note of this problem through a dispatch issued to both Beatty and the Harwich Force that complained of the heavy expenditure of ammunition and torpedoes. This communiqué analyzed the amount of ordnance expended by the ships involved in the raid and contrasted it to the low number of enemy vessels destroyed in the action. The Admiralty concluded that the expenditure was unacceptable and urged greater accuracy in the future.[30] The quality of British shells, however, was the third factor that hampered the effectiveness of the raid; it accounted in part for the heavy expenditure of ammunition with little result. Many British shells failed to explode, as in the case of a shell found intact in the light cruiser

Frauenlob once it arrived back in the port of Wilhelmshaven after the battle. One German account asserts that the Germans believed only half of the British shells had actually detonated during the battle.[31] While this amount of unexploded ordnance seems rather high, it is clear from the accounts of German officers involved in the battle that many British shells indeed did not explode, while several others broke up on impact. The British would suffer similar problems in the 1916 Battle of Jutland. Aside from the quality of shells and deficits in British gunnery, another reason behind the relatively small amount of material damage inflicted in the raid was the structural hardiness of the German warships in general. Of the German vessels sunk, both the *Mainz* and *V-187* were scuttled by their crew rather than succumbing solely to damage from British fire. While it is quite clear that these ships would have sunk regardless, the fact that their crews fought the ships to the end and had to speed their way to destruction is a tribute to German design.

Given these problems, the British owed their success in the Battle of Heligoland Bight in large part to the Germans themselves. Among the factors on the German side that contributed to British victory was a technological consideration. All German warships involved in the engagement were outgunned by their British counterparts. In the case of the cruisers, the primary weapon of the German light cruisers was the 4.1-inch gun, while many British craft shipped 6-inch guns as well as smaller weapons. German ships normally carried greater numbers of these guns than did some of the British craft. For example, the light cruiser *Frauenlob* shipped ten 4.1-inch pieces versus the two 6-inch guns and six 4-inch guns of the British light cruiser *Arethusa*.[32] Two factors in German naval construction accounted for the large numbers of smaller caliber guns relative to the British. The guiding tenet of German naval design was to produce well-balanced ships in terms of fighting ability and the capacity to absorb large amounts of damage. Smaller guns allowed for distribution of the weight to other specifications in order to produce a well-balanced warship. The Germans also placed great emphasis on light cruisers armed with a large number of smaller guns for a tactical reason. The German naval high command mandated that a light cruiser must be able to attack two enemy destroyers at once in defense of the battle fleet.[33] This stipulation did indeed allow the German light cruisers to repel destroyers quite effectively, as in the case of the *Mainz* versus several British torpedo boats. While the German vessel did suffer a torpedo hit, several of the destroyers received damage from the many guns of the German craft. The numbers of the guns, however, meant little in the context of destructive power versus enemy light cruisers. German light cruisers were at a disadvantage when they confronted British light cruisers armed with 6-inch guns. Not only did British ships have an advantage in range, but their shells were also generally larger. A 6-inch British shell weighed one hundred pounds versus the thirty-five pounds of a German 4.1-inch shell.[34] The advantage in the size of the shell was most obvious in the engagement when the *Mainz* fell in with the light cruisers of Goodenough's force. The British commodore's flagship, the *Southampton*, mounted eight 6-inch guns. Clearly, the German cruisers were outmatched by those of Britain.

The same conclusion regarding fighting strength holds true for the German torpedo boats involved in the battle. All of them were outclassed by the British destroyers. German pre-war construction emphasized the belief that the prime purpose of these craft was torpedo attack. As a result, a vessel such as *V-187* carried only two 3.5-inch guns and four 19.7-inch torpedo tubes.[35] The belief in torpedo attack as the chief task of their light craft accounts for the Germans' labeling them "torpedo boats." The British, however, designed their light vessels to attack and destroy enemy torpedo craft. The label of "destroyer" reflects this intention, as the original term for such ships in Britain was "torpedo boat destroyer." The design of a British destroyer, consequently, yielded a craft superior in fighting ability to the German model. The destroyer *Laertes*, for example, mounted three 4-inch guns and four 21-inch torpedo tubes. As a result, the British destroyers were able to throw three times the weight of shell that the German craft could bring to bear.[36]

Far greater than these technological considerations contributing to the relatively poor showing of German forces were tactical ones. Among these was the problem of communication, which greatly hampered the German reaction to events in the bight. Aside from their transmissions being jammed, the delay in decoding messages, the failure to make all commanders fully aware of intelligence on the composition and position of British forces, and poor reporting in general were to blame. The naval high command proved incapable of fast, effective action. Also, the German reaction to the raid was not coordinated well and contributed greatly to German losses in the battle as the British were able to engage and destroy ships piecemeal. The blame for this should rest only in part with Hipper and Maas, the commanders involved in defense of the bight. While they should have ordered the cruisers to deliver a combined assault, which would have produced better results, their actions were guided in part by poor intelligence that did not provide them with information on the presence of a large number of cruisers or battle cruisers until late in the contest. Their actions were also guided by the basic German assumption that the British would not deploy large ships such as battle cruisers in support of light forces in an action in the bight.

Not only Hipper and Maas believed in this assumption, but also commander in chief of the High Seas Fleet Admiral Friedrich von Ingenohl, who must also shoulder blame for the outcome of the battle. This extends past his mistaken belief that the British would not sortie their heavy units into the bight. Ingenohl's desire to preserve the heavy units of the High Seas Fleet rested on the war orders given to him that the fleet must be preserved and face battle only under favorable circumstances, but it prevented the ships from providing any aid to the patrols at Heligoland. His decision to anchor the major units of the fleet off Wilhelmshaven behind the Jade Bar removed them as a factor in the German defense, as the tides did not allow them to sortie over the Jade Bar until late in the battle. Even if heavy units had been outside the Jade Bar, however, they would not have been able to aid the German patrols. Ingenohl's orders to Hipper concerning the use of the battle cruisers typified the cautious nature of the high command, as well as of the politicians, which included the kaiser, on the use of the fleet. By the time Hipper was cleared to enter the bight, his actions were still handicapped by the instructions to avoid any contest against enemy battle cruisers. All told, the war orders of the fleet ran counter to any effective defense against attack. Germany was forced to defend the bight without the aid of its best ships.

The Germans fully appreciated the problems in the defense of the bight. A tactical analysis of the Battle of Heligoland Bight occupied the attention of the naval high command almost immediately after the conclusion of the contest. Repercussions came quickly following more detailed news provided by Hipper on the night of 28 August about the British operation and the German loss of V-187 and the *Ariadne*. A further report on 29 August revealed the destruction of the *Köln* and the *Mainz* to the high command. Admiral von Ingenohl tried to paint the battle in the most favorable light possible when he cabled Kaiser Wilhelm II concerning the loss of the warships. Ingenohl blamed the poor weather, but more attributed the destruction that resulted from the piecemeal engagement of the light cruisers to "the long suppressed battle ardor and the indomitable will of your Majesty's ships to get at the enemy."[37] This explanation did little to assuage the situation as criticism on the conduct of the battle surfaced from both naval and political sources.

A great deal of the criticism came from Admiral von Tirpitz and was directed primarily at Vice Admiral Hipper due to his being charged with the defense of the bight. Tirpitz's reaction came quickly in a letter on 28 August: "I am greatly distressed by the affair in Heligoland. It seems to me that they let themselves be surprised. Our light fighting forces are not sufficient for such skirmishes."[38] The comment on the capability of German light forces indicates the focus of Tirpitz's criticism. The admiral attributed British success to the piecemeal employment of the light cruisers and the failure to deploy major units of the battle fleet in the defense. The fact that his son, Wolf, was captured in the contest probably fueled the admiral's attacks. On 29 August, Tirpitz, at this point not knowing whether Wolf was alive, wrote, "I can scarcely hope that Wolf is among the few saved from the *Mainz*; circumstances were too little in their favor. The small cruisers were too reckless."[39] On the same day as he penned this letter, Tirpitz also wrote to chief of the Admiral Staff Admiral Hugo von Pohl. Tirpitz believed that a great opportunity had been wasted. In his mind, on the first report of British ships in the bight, the German fleet should have sortied not only the light cruisers, but also the battle fleet in order to destroy a portion of the British fleet, in keeping with the German pre-war strategy that called for small engagements to negate Britain's naval superiority over Germany. Tirpitz railed against Hipper's decision to use the light cruisers piecemeal in the bight and unsupported. His stance overlooked the facts that intelligence was poor during the battle through communication difficulties and that the geographic problem of the Jade Bar prevented heavy ships from leaving Wilhelmshaven for much of the battle. Nevertheless, Tirpitz echoed the same assertion on 29 August to Kaiser Wilhelm II. These criticisms fell most heavily on Hipper, as the officer in charge of the defense of the bight, whom Tirpitz eventually held directly responsible for the loss in the battle. Admiral von Pohl shared the belief that Hipper was to blame, while Admiral von Ingenohl supported his subordinate.

For his part, Hipper felt the criticism as well as the outcome of the Battle of Heligoland Bight most keenly and took measures to ensure a better defense in the future. Hipper believed that the lack of heavy ships in support of the bight defenses had been a major problem. He blamed Ingenohl for this situation, as in early August the commander in chief of the High Seas Fleet had refused Hipper's request to attach a battle cruiser to the defense of the bight, in keeping with the high command's desire to protect that fleet from great loss. This belief, however, was a private one and does not appear to have surfaced in any official correspondence regarding the defense of the bight. Hipper reworked the defense to provide for heavy ships that could indeed support the bight. For the rest of the war, at least four capital ships were stationed outside the Jade Bar, while the rest of the battle fleet would be held in a state of readiness for deployment within two hours notice of a raid. Also, to guard against the piecemeal deployment of light cruisers, Hipper mandated that all light cruisers in a raid would retire underneath the guns of Heligoland. Finally, Hipper suggested that two minefields be laid west of Heligoland to augment the defense. These were laid down in mid-September. Ingenohl agreed to all of these steps, as he believed that it was the best defense to guard against a future British raid. He also held that another such action was inevitable. Ingenohl wrote to the kaiser concerning the battle that "[w]ith similar weather and visibility conditions we must reckon with the repetition of such, or similar, undertakings. We must take such measures that no attack objectives worth mentioning will fall prey to enemy superiority in such advances before the decisive battle, if the nature of the undertaking is not such a one as to require full employment of all forces, as for instance, an attempt to block the Jade or similar operations."[40] In effect, the new defense of the bight advocated the use of the fleet in the same way as that advocated at the beginning of the war. The German High Seas Fleet would continue to seek battle only under favorable circumstances in order to pursue the equalization of strength with the British that was necessary for a chance of success in defeating the enemy in a decisive battle.

Ingenohl's justification for the new defense suggests the great importance of the Battle of Heligoland Bight. Rather than being a battle that had a direct material effect on the outcome of the war, the British operation affected the conflict through the morale blow that it delivered to the Germans. The British themselves recognized this fact in subsequent years. Captain Chatfield of the British battle cruiser *Lion* wrote of the battle that "[i]t was no great naval feat, but actually carried out under the nose of the German Commander-in-Chief it actually meant a good deal to Germany and to England."[41] Winston Churchill expounded on this statement in his comments on the battle when he noted the impact on the enemy's morale. These assessments were quite correct. The impact on German politicians and many naval officials is best exhibited in the German official history of the war at sea:

> The 28th of August had shown that the British would come, if at all, only with fast and heavy forces. Thus if [our] own battle cruisers or a squadron of battleships were now sent out to support [our] own scouts at sea, an action of capital ships could develop at any time. It would be difficult to break off such an engagement after damage had been received. In such an event, however, the participation of further squadrons was inevitable, and a battle would ensue, perhaps under conditions unfavorable to us. . . . Thus it came about that the capital ships were held back.[42]

The execution of naval strategy on the basis of this belief had a decisive effect on the war at sea.

The Battle of Heligoland Bight led to an even greater emphasis on the cautious use of the fleet in the war at sea as it confirmed German politicians' pre-war belief in the superiority of the British navy versus Germany's, a belief from which the pre-war plans had developed. The kaiser felt justified in his orders to the fleet at the beginning of the war to seek battle against the British only under favorable circumstances. In addition, Chancellor Bethmann-Hollweg's assertion that the fleet should be used as a bargaining chip for peace negotiations, a belief shared by the kaiser, was entrenched by losses at the Battle of Heligoland Bight. The destruction of four German warships revealed the possibility of a threat to the fleet through potential future loss in the same kind of operation. The battle led the kaiser to put still greater restrictions on the use of the navy when he summoned Pohl and gave new orders on the deployment of the fleet. Pohl subsequently passed these to Ingenohl in a letter that stated, "After that outpost action, His Majesty feared that the fleet might engage a superior enemy, just as the light cruisers had done. In his anxiety to preserve the fleet, he wished you to wire for his consent before entering decisive action."[43] In addition, he not only confined the operations of the High Seas Fleet to the bight, but also directed that even in the bight the bulk of the fleet could not contest any enemy fleet of superior power. The kaiser was within his rights as supreme commander of all Germany's military forces through the German constitution, but his new directive had great ramifications. The operations of the High Seas Fleet were even more greatly curtailed than they had been originally through the first war orders.

Many officials within the German navy recognized that the new order virtually consigned the High Seas Fleet to inactivity for the war and, by extension, assured the loss of the war at sea. The cautious nature of the kaiser would hardly allow for the deployment of the fleet. Tirpitz, the creator of the High Seas Fleet, was one of the most vocal critics of this decision. In his memoirs, the admiral asserted that the "one cause of the navy's tragic fate . . . is to be found in the obstacles placed in the way of its active employment throughout the war for political reasons."[44] The admiral's protestations, according to him, formed the reason behind the erosion of his relationship with the kaiser. These did not sway the mind of Wilhelm II, although an audience with Admiral von Pohl on 4 September 1914, produced an apparent relaxation of the new policy. Pohl, like Tirpitz believed that the new order was a poor one. At this meeting, Pohl delivered a speech entitled "To what extent should the Commander of the High Seas Fleet be limited in his offensive engagements?"[45] In response, the kaiser agreed that the High Seas Fleet should not be restricted any more than what was stated in the original war orders.

Even so, the kaiser's own stance on the use of the navy actually remained that of his new directive that hampered the actions of the navy. Throughout the rest of the war, the kaiser held very tight reign over the High Seas Fleet.[46] Examples are numerous. In October 1914, Wilhelm II ordered the High Seas Fleet to avoid battle under any circumstances. In January 1915, the kaiser cancelled this policy, but granted Ingenohl permission to sortie in the North Sea with the object of destroying only isolated, individual units of the Grand Fleet, in keeping with pre-war strategy. While the kaiser in March 1915 allowed limited operations against larger portions of the Grand Fleet five months later he directed that the deployment of the entire fleet in such an action could be done only with his express permission. Even as late as May 1917, the kaiser permitted operations against portions of the Grand Fleet, but ordered that an action involving all of the fleet could only be authorized by him alone.

The result of the kaiser's decree was twofold in its effect on the war at sea and the war in general. First, it served to greatly reduce the possibility of the decisive naval engagement that both Germany and Britain had envisioned before the war and expected upon its outbreak. This effect quickly became apparent when the British launched another raid into Heligoland Bight on 9 September 1914 that included six battle cruisers. This force steamed to within twelve miles of Heligoland, but encountered no enemy vessels. A further operation planned on

28 September 1914 by Keyes and Tyrwhitt was cancelled before it ever began owing to reports of the new minefields in the bight. The aborted plan prompted Tyrwhitt to write, "We, the Navy, are not doing much, but if the Germans won't come out, what can we do?"[47] This comment was born out of frustration over the return to inaction in the wake of the Battle of Heligoland Bight as little developed in its immediate wake in the war at sea. The High Seas Fleet, more than before the battle, was not inclined to seek a pitched engagement even off its own shores.

The Battle of Heligoland Bight led to a naval war in World War I that increasingly centered on the use of light craft or battle cruisers involved in limited operations as the battleships of the German High Seas Fleet rarely sortied in strength. It entrenched to a far greater degree than before the Germans' defensive mindset in terms of strategy. The Germans pursued, rather than large engagements, actions that could result in whittling away British numerical superiority without risking any of the major units of the battle fleet. Minelayers and submarines accounted for part of the effort. The Germans did employ their battle cruisers to bombard British coastal cities in the wake of the battle in the bight. They also tried to entice a portion of the Royal Navy to sea in order to overwhelm and destroy it. Such efforts produced little result. Indeed, the practice of using the battle cruisers was further curtailed with the 24 January 1915 Battle of Dogger Bank, where a German force under Hipper that included three battle cruisers was intercepted by a squadron under Beatty that included five battle cruisers. By the end of the war, only one fleet engagement, the 1916 Battle of Jutland, had occurred, and this proved indecisive. Throughout the war, the majority of action after the battle of the bight centered on the British naval blockade of Germany and increasingly on the German use of submarines in an attempt to establish a counter blockade against Britain.

Wedded to this problem and exacerbating it was the confusion that reigned throughout the war in the German naval command over the strategy to pursue against Britain. It was quite apparent to the Germans early in the war that the British were not pursuing the strategy of close blockade, upon which the response of Germany was based. The Germans, however, did not have a solution to the problem of breaking Britain's naval superiority in the North Sea. The kaiser's directive after the Battle of Heligoland Bight merely entrenched what was an inadequate strategy, making a solution all the more difficult to find. The Germans did not produce a solution to their strategic dilemma during the war.

The inaction of the fleet, made far more common by the Battle of Heligoland Bight, produced the wider ramification that made the battle a decisive encounter in World War I. Although no naval officials in either Britain or Germany could have fully appreciated this at the time, the battle ensured command of the sea for Britain as it entrenched the German idea of the defensive and shaped future British actions in the war at sea. Such battles as those of Dogger Bank and Jutland merely provided further reinforcement to Germany to remain on the naval defensive. Germany could not afford this stance. As scholars in the past have suggested, only offensive sorties early in the war by the bulk of the High Seas Fleet could have broken Britain's naval supremacy in the North Sea. The restrictions on the German fleet, particularly after the Battle of Heligoland Bight, ensured that the Germans would never break Britain's naval dominance, as the Grand Fleet cruised in the northern portion of the North Sea. This British action was also in part the result of the Battle of Heligoland Bight. On 30 October 1914, commander in chief of the Grand Fleet Admiral Jellicoe issued his estimation of the conduct of the German navy in the wake of the Battle of Heligoland Bight. Jellicoe wrote that

> experience of German methods makes it possible to consider the manner in which they [German warships] are likely to be used tactically in a fleet action. They rely to a great extent on submarines, mines and torpedoes, and they will endeavour to make the fullest use of these. However, they cannot rely on having their full complement of submarines and minelayers in a fleet action unless the battle is fought in the southern North Sea. My object will therefore be to fight the fleet action in the northern part of the North Sea.[48]

This conclusion meant that no fleet action would occur, because the strategies of the two sides were opposed to one another and obviated the chance of a major engagement.

As a result, the British blockade of Germany remained in effect and increased in effectiveness throughout the war. The naval blockade of Germany is a chief reason for the defeat of the country in World War I. It took a massive toll on both the domestic front and military effort on land as the German war effort suffered from lack of food and supplies. The lack of food was one of the greatest problems for the Germans. By 1918, due to the lack of fertilizer and fodder to nourish the soil and animals, Germany's agricultural capacity stood at the same level it had been in the period between 1881 and 1883.[49] The German diet also suffered dramatically from increasingly less supplies from the neutral powers, who by 1918 could no longer export a great deal of supplies to Germany. The British rationed these neutral powers by letting only enough supplies reach them through the blockade as they needed to sustain their home fronts. The lack of food on the home front translated to a lack of the same within the German armies, which decreased their effectiveness in the face of the allied powers. In addition, these armies also suffered from an inadequate supply of the raw industrial materials necessary for war.[50]

The German navy as a result bears a significant portion of the blame for Germany's loss in World War I. The inaction of the German High Seas Fleet automatically surrendered to Britain the command of the sea that Germany needed to contest in order to survive. The fleet orders at the beginning of the war, which stressed battle only under favorable circumstances, were definitely a collective factor in the outcome of the war at sea. The Battle of Heligoland Bight, however, served to take the definition of "favorable circumstances" to the extreme. In the German official history, the author wrote that "the authorities responsible for the use of the fleet . . . must anew consider the question so important in the case of every strategic defensive. Where may I strike without risking too much, and where and when must I strike even at the risk of being annihilated?"[51] Germany was never able to answer these questions. Far more than the material consequences in terms of ships lost, the Battle of Heligoland Bight was a decisive naval contest because it served to make the answer to these questions all the more difficult. The lack of a solution accounts for the actions of the High Seas Fleet that led to its ultimate defeat and that of Germany.

NOTES

1. THE CONTEXT OF THE BATTLE OF HELIGOLAND BIGHT

1. James L. Stokesbury, *Navy and Empire* (New York: William and Morrow, 1983), 280–282.

2. Eric W. Osborne, *Cruisers and Battle Cruisers* (Santa Barbara, Calif.: ABC-CLIO, 2004), 75.

3. Great Britain, Public Record Office, "The Strategic Aspect of Our Building Program," 20 July 1905, CAB 37/81/173 (PRO).

4. Great Britain, Public Record Office, "Strategic Considerations Regarding France and Russia," 1901, CAB 38/1/4 (PRO), 31.

5. Ibid., 33.

6. Holger H. Herwig, *Luxury Fleet: The Imperial German Navy, 1888–1918* (London: George Allen and Unwin, 1980), 13.

7. For an overview of this document, see Terrell D. Gottshall, *By Order of the Kaiser: Otto von Diederichs and the Rise of the Imperial German Navy, 1865–1902* (Annapolis: Naval Institute Press, 2003), 100–101. For the original document, see Denkschrift betreffend die weitere Entwickelung der Kaiserliche Marine, 5 December 1883, BAMA, RM 1/1848.

8. Roger Chesneau and Eugene Kolesnik, eds., *Conway's All the World's Fighting Ships, 1860–1905* (London: Conway Maritime Press, 1979), 242–263.

9. Lamar Cecil, *Wilhelm II*, vol. 2: *Emperor and Exile 1900–1941* (Chapel Hill: University of North Carolina Press, 1996), 86.

10. Herwig, *Luxury Fleet*, 17.

11. Jonathan Steinberg, *Yesterday's Deterrent: Tirpitz and the Birth of the German Battle Fleet* (New York: Macmillan, 1965), 209–221.

12. Paul Kennedy, "The Development of German Naval Operations: Plans against England, 1896–1914," *English Historical Review*, vol. 89, no. 350 (January 1974): 55.

13. Tirpitz, *Politische Dokumente*, vol. 1 (Stuttgart, Germany: 1924), 462–463.

14. Wilhelm Deist, *Flottenpolitik und Flottenpropaganda: Das Nachrichtenbureau des Reichsmarineamtes, 1897–1914* (Stuttgart, Germany: Deutsche Verlagsanstalt, 1976), 157.

15. Tirpitz, *Politische Dokumente*, 462–463.

16. Eric W. Osborne, *Britain's Economic Blockade of Germany, 1914–1919* (London: Frank Cass, 2004), 20.

17. G. P. Gooch and Harold Temperley, eds., *British Documents on the Origins of the War, 1898–1914*. Vol. 6: *Anglo-German Tension: Armaments and Negotiation, 1907–1912*. London: HMSO, 1930.

18. Ernest L. Woodward, *Great Britain and the German Navy* (New York: Clarendon Press, 1935), 374.

19. Herwig, *Luxury Fleet*, 59, 70.

20. Winston Churchill, *The World Crisis: 1911–1914*, vol. 1 (London: Thornton Butterworth, 1923), 95.

21. Paul Halpern, *A Naval History of World War I* (Annapolis: Naval Institute Press, 1994), 7–8.

22. Gottschall, 121.

23. Great Britain, Foreign Office, Historical Section, *The Kiel Canal and Heligoland*, Handbook Prepared under the Direction of the Historical Section of the Foreign Office, No. 41 (London: HMSO, 1920), 4.

24. George Drower, *Heligoland: The True Story of German Bight and the Island That Britain Betrayed* (Thrupp, Stroud, Gloucestershire, England: Sutton, 2002), 116.

25. Arthur Marder, *From the Dreadnought to Scapa Flow: The Royal Navy in the Fisher Era, 1904–1919*, vol. 1: *The Road to War, 1904–1910* (London: Oxford University Press, 1961), 367.

26. W. R. Robertson, in Great Britain, Public Record Office, "The Military Resources of Germany, and Probable Method of Their Employment in a War between Germany and England," p. 1, 7 February 1903, CAB 38/4/9 (PRO).

27. E. A. Altham, in Great Britain, Public Record Office, "Memorandum on the Military Policy to Be Adopted in a War with Germany," 10 February 1903, p. 8, CAB 38/4/9 (PRO).

28. Halpern, *Naval History*, 21.

29. Nicholas Lambert, "British Naval Policy, 1913–1914: Financial Limitations and Strategic Revolution," *Journal of Modern History* 67 (September 1995): 600. See also John Beeler, *British Naval Policy in the Gladstone-Disraeli Era, 1866–1880* (Stanford, Calif.: Stanford University Press, 1997), 212. See also Osborne, *Britain's Economic Blockade of Germany*, 45.

30. Great Britain, Public Record Office, "Minutes of the 114th meeting of the Committee of Imperial Defense," pp. 11–15, 23 August 1911, CAB 2/2 (PRO).

31. Andrew Lambert, "Admiral Sir Arthur Knyvett-Wilson, V.C. (1910–1911)," in Malcolm Murfett, ed., *The First Sea Lords: From Fisher to Mountbatten* (London: Praeger, 1995), 49.

32. Osborne, *Britain's Economic Blockade of Germany*, 49.

33. Drower, 155–156.

34. Marder, *Road to War*, 256–257.

35. Gottschall, 124–125.

36. Ibid., 284.

37. Ibid., 126.

38. Ibid., 127.

39. Kennedy, "The Development of German Naval Operations," p. 51.

40. "Immediatvortrang Betreffend Grundzüge für einen Operationsplan Deutschlands allein gegen England allein," 31 May 1897, BAMA, F. 5587, III. 1. no.10, vol. 1.

41. Jonathan Steinberg, "A German Plan for the Invasion of Holland and Belgium, 1897," *Historical Journal* 6, no. 1 (1963): 107–119.

42. Kennedy, "The Development of German Naval Operations," 54.

43. Ibid., 72.

44. Otto Groos, *The War in the North Sea, 1914–1918*, vol. 1, *From the Beginning of the War to the First of September 1914*, part 1, ch. "Considerations for the Operation Orders," trans. R. E. Krause (Newport, R.I.: Naval War College, 1934), 78.

45. Gerhard Ritter, *The Sword and the Scepter: The Problem of Militarism in Germany*, vol. 2: *The European Powers and the Wilhelminian Empire, 1890–1914*, trans. Heinz Norden (Coral Gables, Fla.: University of Miami Press, 1970), 149.

46. Bendemann, "Die Defensive gegen England," BAMA, F 5587, III, no. 10, vol. 1.

47. Paul Kennedy, ed., *The War Plans of the Great Powers, 1880–1914* (London: George Allen and Unwin, 1979), 178.

48. Marder, *Road to War*, 42.

49. Kennedy, *Development of German Naval Operations*, 63.

50. Groos, "Considerations for the Operation Orders," 88.

51. Memorandum from Admiralty Staff to Wilhelm II, 10 August 1910, BAMA, F. 5587, III, 1.N.10, vol. 5.

52. Groos, "Considerations for the Operation Orders," 90.

53. Erich Raeder, *My Life*, trans. Henry W. Drexel (Annapolis: Naval Institute Press, 1960), 40.

54. Holger Herwig, "The Failure of German Sea Power, 1914–1945: Mahan, Tirpitz, and Raeder Reconsidered," *International History Review* 10, no. 1 (February 1988): 81.

55. Reinhard Scheer, *Germany's High Seas Fleet in the World War* (London: Cassell, 1920), 11.

56. Halpern, *Naval History*, 23.

57. For a thorough account of the history of the Admiralty, see N. A. M. Rodger, *The Admiralty* (London: Terence Dalton, 1979).

58. Winston Churchill, 92. See also Richard Hough, *The Great War at Sea, 1914–1918* (Oxford: Oxford University Press, 1983), 34.

59. Randolph Churchill and Martin Gilbert, *Winston S. Churchill*, vol. 2 (Boston: Houghton Mifflin, 1967), 1312.

60. Arthur Marder, *From the Dreadnought to Scapa Flow: The Royal Navy in the Fisher Era, 1904–1919*, vol. 2: *The War Years: To the Eve of Jutland* (London: Oxford University Press, 1965), 37.

61. For a detailed analysis of the Naval War Staff, see H. G. Thursfield, *The Naval Staff of the Admiralty*, Naval Staff Monograph (1929).

62. Herwig, *German Naval Officer Corps*, 27.

63. Walther Hubatsch, *Der Admiralstab und die obersten Marinebehörden in Deutschland* (Frankfurt: Verlag für Wehrwesen Bernhard und Graefe, 1958), 35.

64. Scheer, 17.

65. Herwig, *German Naval Officer Corps*, 147.

66. Prince Bernard von Bülow, *Memoirs*, vol. 2 (Boston: Little, Brown, 1932), 36.

67. Scheer, 11.

68. Gerhard Ritter, *The Sword and the Scepter: The Problem of Militarism in Germany*, vol. 3: *The Tragedy of Statesmanship-Bethmann Hollweg as War Chancellor (1914–1917)*, trans. Heinz Norden (Coral Gables, Fla.: University of Miami Press, 1972), 18.

69. William B. Black, *Naval Actions of the First World War*, Study No. 102/80, *Battle of Heligoland Bight, 28th August 1914*. (Lenzie, Dunbartonshire, Scotland: private printing, 1982). Available at the U.S. Navy Department Library, Naval Historical Center.

70. Walter Gorlitz, ed., *The Kaiser and His Court: The Diaries, Note Books, and*

Letters of Admiral Georg Alexander von Müller, Chief of the Naval Cabinet, 1914–1918, trans. Mervyn Savill (New York: Harcourt Brace, 1959), 17.

2. NAVAL OPERATIONS UPON THE OUTBREAK OF WORLD WAR I AND THE GENESIS OF THE PLAN FOR A RAID INTO HELIGOLAND BIGHT

1. Spencer C. Tucker, *The Great War, 1914–1918* (Bloomington: Indiana University Press, 1998), 6.

2. Robert K. Massie, *Castles of Steel: Britain, Germany, and the Winning of the Great War at Sea* (New York: Random House, 2003), 15.

3. Winston Churchill, 212.

4. For a complete account of the disposition of British naval units, see Halpern, *Naval History*, 594–595.

5. Massie, 15.

6. For a complete account of the disposition of German naval units, see Halpern, *Naval History*, 26. See also Scheer, 13–16; James Goldrick, *The King's Ships Were at Sea: The War in the North Sea, August 1914–February 1915* (Annapolis: Naval Institute Press, 1984), 49, 50.

7. Goldrick, 65.

8. Claude Lombard Aubry Woollard, *With the Harwich Naval Forces, 1914 1918; or, Under Commodore Tyrwhitt in the North Sea* (Antwerp: Kohler, 1931), 3.

9. Tucker, 28.

10. A. Temple Patterson, *Tyrwhitt of the Harwich Force: The Life of the Admiral of the Fleet, Sir Reginald Tyrwhitt* (London: MacDonald, 1973), 51.

11. Ritter, 157.

12. Tirpitz, *Politische Dokumente*, 160.

13. Theobald von Schaefer, *General Staff and Admiral Staff: The Cooperation of the German Army and Navy in the World War*, trans. Fred W. Merten (Carlisle, Penn: Army War College, 1937), 25, 26.

14. Alfred von Tirpitz, *My Memoirs*, vol. 2 (New York: Dodd, Mead, 1919), 90–91.

15. Scheer, 11.

16. Roger Keyes, *The Naval Memoirs of Admiral of the Fleet Sir Roger Keyes: The Narrow Seas to the Dardenelles, 1910–1915* (London: Thornton Butterworth, 1934), 70.

17. Bernard Fitzsimons, ed., *Warships and Sea Battles of World War I* (London: Phoebus, 1973), 20.

18. Scheer, 40.

19. Keyes, 75–76.

20. Beatty to his wife, 24 August 1914, in Bryan Ranft, ed., *The Beatty Papers: Selections from the Private and Official Correspondence of Admiral of the Fleet Earl Beatty*, vol. 1: *1902–1918*, Navy Records Society vol. 128 (Aldershot, U.K.: Scholar Press, 1989), 120–121.

21. Görlitz, 22.

22. Daniel Horn, ed., *War Mutiny, and Revolution in the German Navy: The World War I Diary of Seaman Richard Stumpf* (New Brunswick, N.J.: Rutgers University Press, 1967), 27.

23. Cecil Aspinall-Oglander, *Roger Keyes: Being the Biography of Admiral of the Fleet Lord Keyes of Zeebrugge and Dover* (London: Hogarth, 1951), 91.

24. Robert Gardiner, ed., *Conway's All the World's Fighting Ships, 1860–1905* (London: Conway's Maritime Press, 1979), 84. See also Randal Gray, ed., *Conway's All the World's Fighting Ships, 1906–1921* (London: Conway Maritime Press, 1985), 75, 76.

25. Keyes to his wife, 1 August 1914, in Paul G. Halpern, ed., *The Keyes Papers: Selections from the Private and Official Correspondence of Admiral of the Fleet Baron Keyes of Zeebrugge*, vol. 1: *1914–1918*, Navy Records Society vol. 117 (London: William Clowes, 1972), 8.

26. Patterson, *Tyrwhitt of the Harwich Forces*, 43.

27. Ibid., 52.

28. Scheer, 11.

29. Keyes to Leveson, 23 August 1914, in Halpern, *Keyes Papers*, 9–10.

30. *PersonalAkten Hipper*, BAMA, *Qualificationsberichte*, No. 37, May 1914.

31. For full information on the defenses of Heligoland Bight, see Otto Groos, *The War in the North Sea*, vol. 1: *From the Beginning of the War to the First of September 1914*, part 2, ch. 5, "The 28th August 1914," trans. R. E. Kreuse (Newport, R.I.: Naval War College, 1937), 10–18.

32. Ibid., 12.

33. Raeder, 46.

34. Keyes to Leveson, 23 August 1914, in Halpern, *Keyes Papers*, 10.

35. Keyes, 81.

36. Arthur Marder, *Portrait of an Admiral: The Life and Papers of Sir Herbert Richmond* (Cambridge, Mass.: Harvard University Press, 1952), 98.

37. Hough, 147–148.

38. Jellicoe to Admiralty, 18 August 1914, in A. Temple Patterson, ed., *The Jellicoe Papers: Selections from the Private and Official Correspondence of Admiral of the Fleet Earl Jellicoe of Scapa*, vol. 1: *1893–1916* (London: Spottiswoode, Ballantyne, 1967), 50.

39. Julian Corbett, *History of the Great War Based on Official Documents: Naval Operations*, vol. 1: *To the Battle of the Falklands, December 1914* (New York: Longmans, Green, 1920), 103.

40. Goldrick, 84–85.

41. For details on the disposition of submarines in the operation, see Corbett, 103. See also Black, 4.

42. Great Britain, Admiralty, *Official Naval Dispatches: The Admiralty's Reports of the Battle of the Bight, Destruction of German East Asiatic Squadron, Sinking of the Emden, and Other Work of the Navy in the War* (London: Graphic, 1919), 20. Rear Admiral Christian's after-action report for the Battle of Heligoland Bight is quite brief, reflecting the fact that he took no great part in the battle.

43. Keyes, 77.

44. Marder, *Portrait of an Admiral*, 103.

45. Admiralty to Jellicoe, 26 August 1914, in Great Britain, Admiralty, *Battle of Heligoland Bight, August 28th 1914*, Naval Staff Monograph (Historical), vol. 3, no. 11 (CB 1585) (1921), 149.

46. John Jellicoe, *The Grand Fleet, 1914–1916: Its Creation, Development, and Work* (New York: George H. Doran, 1919), 109.

47. Jellicoe to Admiralty, 26 August 1914, *Battle of Heligoland Bight*, 149.

48. Admiralty to Jellicoe, 27 August 1914, ibid.

3. THE COMMENCEMENT OF THE BATTLE OF HELIGOLAND BIGHT

1. For details concerning the beginning of Keyes's sortie, see Great Britain, Admiralty, *Official Naval Dispatches*, 24. For complete technical details of forces under Keyes's command, see Gray, 75, 87–88.

2. Great Britain, Admiralty, *The Battle of "The Bight": Being the Official Narrative of the Naval Engagement between the British and the German Fleets in the Heligoland Bight on Friday, August 28th, 1914* (London: Yachting Monthly, 1914), 4.

3. Osborne, *Cruisers and Battle Cruisers*, 208.

4. Patterson, *Tyrwhitt of the Harwich Forces*, 54.

5. Ibid.

6. For technical specifications, see Gray, 75–76.

7. Ibid., 24.

8. Gardiner, 68.

9. Osborne, *Cruisers and Battle Cruisers*, 207.

10. For full technical specifications of all of the vessels in the First Light Cruiser Squadron, see Gray, 51–54.

11. W. S. Chalmers, *The Life and Letters of David Earl Beatty* (London: Hodder and Stoughton, 1951), 143. See also Beatty to Battle Cruiser Force, 27 August 1914, in Great Britain, Admiralty, *Battle of Heligoland Bight, August 28th 1914*, Naval Staff Monograph (Historical), vol. 3, no. 11 (CB 1585) (1921), 149.

12. Black, 7.

13. Ibid., 6.

14. Keyes, 82.

15. Gray, 166–167.

16. Gardiner, 264–265.

17. See Gray, 157. See also Gardiner, 258.

18. For force disposition, see Groos, "The 28th August," 22.

19. Ibid., 20.

20. Gray, 151–153.

21. Groos, 23.

22. Ibid., 16. See also Drower, 134, 158.

23. Otto Groos, *The War in the North Sea*, vol. 1: *From the Beginning of the War to the First of September* 1914, appendix 21, "Compilation of the German Wireless Messages of the 28 August 1914," trans. Walter Hibbs (Newport, R.I.: Naval War College, 1935), 178.

24. Ibid., 179.

25. This assertion seems to stem from the British official history of the war, see Corbett, 105. The German official history accounts the action of their torpedo boats as being those of captains caught completely by surprise in search of help.

26. Groos, "The 28th August, 1914," 27.

27. Groos, "Compilation of German Wireless Messages, 28 August, 1914," 179.

28. Groos, "The 28th August, 1914," 30.

29. Groos, "Compilation of German Wireless Messages, 28 August, 1914," 180.

30. Black, 13.

31. Goldrick, 90.

32. Groos, "The 28th August, 1914," 36.

33. Goldrick, 88.

34. Black, 15.

35. Groos, "The 28th August, 1914," 33.

36. Great Britain, Admiralty, *Official Naval Dispatches*, 21.

37. Woollard, 11.

38. Edward F. Knight, *The Harwich Naval Forces: Their Part in the Great War* (London: Hodder and Stoughton, 1919), 33.

39. Patterson, *Tyrwhitt of the Harwich Forces*, 62.

40. Ibid., 63.

41. *Norges Handels und Sjofaerts Tidende*, 22 September 1914.

42. Great Britain, Admiralty, *Battle of "The Bight,"* 5. Among the most recent books to duplicate this error is Robert Massie in his 2003 book, *Castles of Steel*.

43. Horn, 41.

44. For details of the encounter, see Keyes, 83.

45. Groos, "Compilation of German Wireless Messages, 28 August, 1914," 181.

46. Scheer, 47.

47. Groos, "The 28th August, 1914," 48–49.

48. Scheer, 48.

49. Ibid.

50. Hector C. Bywater, *Cruisers in Battle: Naval Light Cavalry under Fire, 1914–1918* (London: Constable, 1939), 50.

51. Groos, "The 28th August, 1914," 55.

52. Great Britain, Admiralty, *Battle of "The Bight,"* 15.

53. Groos, "The 28th August, 1914," 61.

4. THE BATTLE OF THE BIGHT BECOMES A DECISIVE VICTORY

1. Goldrick, 97.

2. Keyes to Goodenough, 28 August 1914, in Great Britain, Admiralty, *Battle of Heligoland Bight, August 28th 1914*, Naval Staff Monograph (Historical), vol. 3, no. 11 (CB 1585), (1921), 151.

3. Ibid.

4. Ranft, 123.

5. Halpern, ed., *Keyes Papers*, 15.

6. Black, 22.

7. Great Britain, Admiralty, *Battle of Heligoland Bight*, 142.

8. Horn, 38.

9. Groos, "Compilation of German Wireless Messages, 28 August, 1914," 182.

10. Claude Woollard, *With the Harwich Naval Forces, 1914–1918; or, Under Commodore Tyrwhitt in the North Sea* (Antwerp, 1931), 13.

11. Roger Chesneau and Eugene Kolesnik, eds., *Conway's All the World's Fighting Ships, 1860–1905* (London: Conway Maritime Press, 1979), 255.

12. Bryan Ranft, ed., *The Beatty Papers*, vol. I, *1902–1918*, 124.

13. Great Britain, Admiralty, *Official Naval Dispatches: The Admiralty's Reports of the Battle of the Bight, Destruction of the German East Asiatic Squadron, Sinking of the Emden, and Other Work of the Navy in the War* (London: Graphic, 1919), 22.

14. Ranft, 124.

15. Alfred Ernle Chatfield, *The Navy and Defense: The Autobiography of Admiral of the Fleet Lord Chatfield* (London: William Heinemann, 1942), 124.

16. Ibid.

17. Ranft, 124–125.

18. Goldrick, 101.

19. Groos, "The 28th August, 1914," 67.

20. Scheer, 51.

21. Groos, "The 28th August, 1914," 70.

22. Lady L. King-Hall, *Sea Saga* (London: Gollancz, 1935), 382.

23. Groos, "The 28th August, 1914," 69–70.

24. Stephen King-Hall, *A North Sea Diary, 1914–1918* (London: Newnes, 1936), 55–56.

25. For information on this event, see Hugo von Waldeyer-Hartz, *Admiral von Hipper*, trans. F. Appleby Holt (London: Rich and Cowan, 1933), 116–117.

26. Aspinall-Oglander, 95.

27. Waldeyer-Hartz, 117.

28. Bywater, 59.

29. Groos, "Compilation of German Wireless Messages, 28 August, 1914," 187.

30. Marder, *War Years*, 52.

31. Geoffrey Bennett, *Naval Battles of the First World War* (London: B. T. Batsford, 1968), 149.

32. Ranft, 125.

33. Horn, 39.

34. Groos, "Compilation of German Wireless Messages, 28 August, 1914," 180.

35. Chatfield, 125.

36. Bywater, 70.

37. Groos, "The 28th August, 1914," 120.

38. Ibid., 121.

39. Ibid., 88.

5. THE AFTERMATH OF THE BATTLE AND ITS RAMIFICATIONS ON THE WAR AT SEA

1. Groos, "Compilation of German Wireless Messages, 28 August, 1914," 190–193.

2. Ibid., 193–194.

3. Ibid., 195.

4. Groos, "The 28th August, 1914, 95.

5. Black, 36.

6. Beatty to Admiralty, 30 August 1914, in Ranft, 125.

7. For details of the transfer, see Keyes to Chief of the War Staff, 29 August 1914, in Halpern, ed., *Keyes Papers*, 13. For further information see Christian to Admiralty, 28 September 1914, in Great Britain, Admiralty, *Official Naval Dispatches*20.

8. Keyes, *Naval Memoirs of Admiral of the Fleet Sir Roger Keyes*, 89.

9. Patterson, *Tyrwhitt of the Harwich Force*, 61.

10. Ibid., 62.

11. Ibid.

12. Stephen King-Hall, *A North Sea Diary, 1914–1918* (London: Newnes, 1936), 59.

13. Chalmers, 152.

14. Tucker, 50.

15. Groos, "The 28th August, 1914," 104.

16. Keyes, 97.

17. For the *Daily Express* title, see Marder, *War Years*, 54. For the *Times*, see London *Times*, 29 August 1914, p. 1, and London *Times*, 30 August 1914, p. 2.

18. Churchill, 306, 308.

19. Ibid., 308.

20. Ibid., 309.

21. Marder, *Portrait of an Admiral*, 103.

22. Ibid., 104.

23. Keyes to Goodenough, 5 September 1914, in Halpern, *Keyes Papers*, 19.

24. Goodenough to Keyes, 14 September 1914, in Halpern, *Keyes Papers*, 20.

25. William E. Goodenough, *A Rough Record* (London: Hutchinson, 1939), 92.

26. Beatty to his wife, 29 August 1914, in Ranft, 121.

27. Beatty to his wife, 2 September 1914, in Ranft, 132.

28. Goldrick, 113.

29. Marder, *War Years*, 53.

30. Chatfield, 126.

31. Horn, 41. See also Otto Groos, *The War in the North Sea*, vol. 1, *From the Beginning of the War to the First of September 1914*, part 2, ch. 5, 108.

32. See Chesneau and Kolesnik, 258. See also Gray, 55.

33. Groos, "The 28th August 1914," 105.

34. Goldrick, 116.

35. Gray, 166. For a comparison with British destroyer *Laertes*, see also Gray, 76.

36. Goldrick, 115.

37. Groos, "The 28th August, 1914," 110.

38. Tirpitz, 221–222.

39. Ibid., 222.

40. Groos, "The 28th August, 1914," 112.

41. Chatfield, 126.

42. Groos, "The 28th August, 1914," 116–7.

43. Great Britain, Admiralty, *Battle of Heligoland Bight*, 148.

44. Tirpitz, 87.

45. Gorlitz, 28.

46. Holger Herwig, *The German Naval Officer Corps: A Social and Political History, 1890–1918* (Oxford: Clarendon Press, 1973), 178–179.

47. Marder, 55.

48. Bennett, 152.

49. P. Mertz, "The Food Supply of Germany," in John Keynes, ed., *Reconstruction in Europe* (Manchester: Manchester Guardian Commercial, 1922).

50. Osborne, *Britain's Economic Blockade of Germany*, 183.

51. Otto Groos, *The War in the North Sea*, vol. 1: *From the Beginning of the War to the First of September 1914*, part 2, ch. 6, "The British Blockade," trans. W. E. Findeisen (Newport, R.I.: Naval War College, 1935), 162–163.

SELECTED BIBLIOGRAPHY

PRIMARY DOCUMENTS

Bethmann Hollweg, Theobald. *Reflections on the World War*. Trans. George Young. London: Thornton Butterworth, 1920.

Bülow, Bernhard von. *Memoirs*. Vol. 2. Boston: Little, Brown, 1932.

Chatfield, Alfred Ernle Montacute. *The Navy and Defense: The Autobiography of Admiral of the Fleet Lord Chatfield*. London: William Heinemann, 1942.

Churchill, Winston. *The World Crisis, 1911–1914*. Vol. 1. London: Thornton Butterworth, 1923.

Corbett, Julian. *History of the Great War, Based on Official Documents: Naval Operations*. Vol. 1: *To the Battle of the Falklands December 1914*. New York: Longmans, Green, 1920.

Gooch, G. P., and Harold Temperley, eds., *British Documents on the Origins of the War, 1898–1914*. Vol. 6: *Anglo-German Tension: Armaments and Negotiation, 1907–1912*. London: HMSO, 1930.

Goodenough, William E. *A Rough Record*. London: Hutchinson, 1939.

Görlitz, Walter, ed. *The Kaiser and His Court: The Diaries, Note Books, and Letters of Admiral Georg Alexander von Müller, Chief of the Naval Cabinet, 1914–1918*. Trans. Mervyn Savill. New York: Harcourt Brace, 1959.

Germany. Bundesarchiv-Militärarchiv (BAMA). RM 1/1848. "Denkschrift betreffend die weitere Entwickelung der Kaiserliche Marine," 5 December 1883.

_____. F. 5587, III. Number 10. Vol. 1. Bendemen, Felix von. "Die Defensive gegen England."

_____. F. 5587, III. Number 10. Vol. 1. "Immediatvortrang Betreffend Grundzüge für einen Operationsplan Deutschlands allein gegen England allein," 31 May 1897.

_____. F. 5587, III. Number 10. Vol. 1. "Memorandum from Admiralty Staff to Wilhelm II," 10 August 1910.

_____. *PersonalAkten Hipper. Qualificationsberichte*. Number 37. May 1914.

Great Britain. Admiralty. ADM 1/8404/438. "Information obtained by crew of HMS *Arethusa* from German officer on Battle of Heligoland Bight, 27 Nov 1914."

——. *Battle of Heligoland Bight, August 28th 1914*. Naval Staff Monograph No. 11 (CB 1585), 1921.

——. *The Battle of "The Bight," Being the Official Narrative of the Naval Engagement between the British and German Fleets in the Heligoland Bight on Friday, August 28th, 1914*. London: Yachting Monthly, 1914.

——. *Official Naval Dispatches: The Admiralty's Reports of the Battle of the Bight, Destruction of the German East Asiatic Squadron, Sinking of the Emden, and Other Work of the Navy in the War*. London: Graphic, 1919.

Great Britain. Foreign Office. Historical Section. *The Kiel Canal and Helgoland*. Handbook Prepared under the Direction of the Historical Section of the Foreign Office, No. 41. London: HMSO, 1920.

Great Britain. Public Record Office. *ADM 1/8461/450*. "Complaint of Sir David Beatty re Dispatches on Battle of Jutland, Dogger Bank, and Heligoland Bight," 21 June 1916.

——. *ADM 137/1943, 1949, 3139*. "28 Aug 1914 Action in the Bight."

——. *CAB 2/2*. "Minutes of the 114th meeting of the Committee of Imperial Defense," August 1911.

——. *CAB 37/81/173*. "The Strategic Aspect of Our Building Program," 20 July 1905.

——. *CAB 38/1/14*. "Strategic Considerations Regarding France and Russia," 1901.

——. *CAB 38/4/9*. "The Military Resources of Germany, and Probable Method of their Employment in a War between Germany and England," 7 February 1903.

——. *CAB 38/4/9*. "Memorandum on the Military Policy to be Adopted in a War with Germany," 10 February 1903.

Groos, Otto. *The War in the North Sea, 1914–1918*. Vol. 1: *From the Beginning of the War to the First of September* 1914. Part 1, Ch. 2: "Considerations for the Operation Orders." Trans. R. E. Krause. Newport, R.I.: Naval War College, 1934. Available at the Library of the United States Air Force Academy.

——. *The War in the North Sea, 1914–1918*. Vol. 1: *From the Beginning of the War to the First of September* 1914. Part 2, Ch. 5: "The 28th August, 1914." Trans. R. E. Krause. Newport, R.I.: Naval War College, 1934. Available at the Library of the United States Air Force Academy.

——. *The War in the North Sea, 1914–1918*. Vol. 1: *From the Beginning of the War to the First of September* 1914. Part 2, Ch. 6: "The British Blockade." Trans. W. E. Findeisen. Newport, R.I.: Naval War College, 1935. Available at the Library of the United States Air Force Academy.

——. *The War in the North Sea, 1914–1918*. Vol. 1: *From the Beginning of the War to the First of September* 1914. Appendix 21: "Compilation of the German Wireless Messages of the 28 August 1914." Trans. Walter Hibbs. Newport, R.I.: Naval War College, 1935. Available at the Library of the United States Air Force Academy.

Halpern, Paul G., ed. *The Keyes Papers: Selections from the Private and Official Correspondence of Admiral of the Fleet Baron Keyes of Zeebrugge*. Vol. 1: 1914–1918. Navy Records Society vol. 117. London: William Clowes, 1972.

Horn, Daniel, ed. *War, Mutiny, and Revolution in the German Navy: The World War I Diary of Seaman Richard Stumpf*. New Brunswick, N.J.: Rutgers University Press, 1967.

Jellicoe, John. *The Grand Fleet, 1914–1916: Its Creation, Development, and Work*. New York: George H. Doran: 1919.

Keyes, Roger. *The Naval Memoirs of Admiral of the Fleet Sir Roger Keyes: The Narrow Seas to the Dardenelles, 1910–1915*. London: Thornton Butterworth, 1934.

King-Hall, Stephen. *A North Sea Diary, 1914–1918*. London: Newnes, 1936.

Lutz, Ralph Haswell, ed., *Fall of the German Empire, 1914–1918*. Vol. 1. London: Oxford University Press, 1932.

Marder, Arthur. *Portrait of an Admiral: The Life and Papers of Sir Herbert Richmond*. Cambridge, Mass.: Harvard University Press, 1952.

Nationalversammlung. *Official German Documents Relating to the World War*. 2 vols. Translated under supervision of the Carnegie Endowment for International Peace. New York: Oxford University Press, 1923.

Norges Handels und Sjofaerts Tidende, 22 September 1914.

Patterson, A. Temple, ed. *The Jellicoe Papers: Selections from the Private and Official Correspondence of Admiral of the Fleet Earl Jellicoe of Scapa*. Vol. 1: 1893–1916. Navy Records Society vol. 108. London: Spottiswoode, Ballantyne, 1967.

Raeder, Erich. *My Life*. Trans. Henry W. Drexel. Annapolis: Naval Institute Press, 1960.

Ranft, B. *The Beatty Papers: Selections from the Private and Official Correspondence of Admiral of the Fleet Earl Beatty*. Vol. 1: 1902–1918. Navy Records Society vol. 128. Aldershot, U.K.: Scholar Press, 1989.

Scheer, Reinhardt. *Germany's High Sea Fleet in the World War*. London: Cassell, 1920.

Thursfield, H. G. *The Naval Staff of the Admiralty*. Naval Staff Monograph. Admiralty, 1929.

Times (London). 29–31 August 1914.

Tirpitz, Alfred von. *My Memoirs*. Vol. 2. New York: Dodd, Mead, 1919.

———. *Politische Dokumente*. Vol. 1. Stuttgart, Germany: 1924.

United States. National Archives. Record Group 45, Box 802. Naval Records Collection of the Office of Naval Records and Library, 1911–1927.

SECONDARY SOURCES

Aspinall-Oglander, Cecil. *Roger Keyes: Being the Biography of Admiral of the Fleet Lord Keyes of Zeebrugge and Dover*. London: Hograth, 1951.

Beeler, John. *British Naval Policy in the Gladstone-Disraeli Era, 1866–1880*. Stanford, Calif.: Stanford University Press, 1997.

Bennett, Geoffrey. *Naval Battles of the First World War*. London: B. T. Batsford, 1968.

Black, William B. *Naval Actions of the First World War*. Study No. 102/80. *Battle of Heligoland Bight, 28th August 1914*. Private Printing. Lenzie, Dunbartonshire, Scotland, 1982. Available at the U.S. Navy Department Library, Naval Historical Center.

Bradley, Dermot, ed. *Deutschlands Generale und Admirale*. Osnabrück, Germany: Biblio Verlag, 1990.

Bywater, Hector C. *Cruisers in Battle: Naval "Light Cavalry" under Fire, 1914–1918*. London: Constable, 1939.

Campbell, N. J. M. *Jutland: An Analysis of the Fighting*. London: Conway Maritime Press, 1986.

Carr, William. *Brass Hats and Bell Bottomed Trousers: Unforgettable and Splendid Feats of the Harwich Patrol*. London: Hutchinson, 1939.

Cecil, Lamar. *Wilhelm II*. Vol. 2: *Emperor and Exile, 1900–1941*. Chapel Hill: University of North Carolina Press, 1996.

Chalmers, W. S. *The Life and Letters of David Earl Beatty*. London: Hodder and Stoughton, 1951.

Chesneau, Roger, and Eugene Kolesnik, eds. *Conway's All the World's Fighting Ships, 1860–1905*. London: Conway Maritime Press, 1979.

Chickering, Roger. *Imperial Germany and the Great War, 1914–1918*. Cambridge, Cambridge University Press, 1998.

Churchill, Randolph and Martin Gilbert. *Winston S. Churchill*. Vol. 2. Boston: Houghton Mifflin, 1967.

Deist, Wilhelm. *Flottenpolitik und Flottenpropaganda: Das Nachrichtenbureau des Reichsmarineamtes, 1897–1914*. Stuttgart, Germany: Deutsche Verlagsanstalt, 1976.

Dorling, Taprell. *Endless Story: Being an Account of the World of the Destroyers, Flotilla-Leaders, Torpedo-Boats, and Patrol Boats in the Great War*. London: Hodder and Stoughton, 1931.

Drower, George. *Heligoland: The True Story of German Bight and the Island that Britain Betrayed*. Thrupp, Stroud, Gloucestershire, U.K.: Sutton, 2002.

Edwards, Bernard. *Salvo! Classic Naval Gun Actions*. Annapolis: Naval Institute Press, 1995.

Fischer, Jörg-Uwe. *Admiral des Kaisers: Georg Alexander von Müller als Chef des Marinekabinetts Wilhelms II*. New York: Peter Lang, 1992.

Fitzsimons, Bernard, ed. *Warships and Sea Battles of World War I*. London: Phoebus, 1973.

Frothingham, Thomas G. *The Naval History of the World War: Offensive Operations, 1914–1915*. Cambridge, Mass.: Harvard University Press, 1924.

Gardiner, Robert, ed. *Conway's All the World's Fighting Ships, 1860–1905*. London: Conway's Maritime Press, 1979.

George, James L. *History of Warships: From Ancient Times to the Twenty-First Century*. Annapolis: Naval Institute Press, 1998.

Gillard, D. R. "Salisbury's African Policy and the Heligoland Offer of 1890." *English Historical Review* 75, no. 297 (October 1960): 631–653.

Goldrick, James. *The King's Ships Were at Sea: The War in the North Sea, August 1914–February 1915*. Annapolis: Naval Institute Press, 1984.

Gottschall, Terrell. *By Order of the Kaiser: Otto von Diederichs and the Rise of the Imperial German Navy, 1865–1902*. Annapolis: Naval Institute Press, 2003.

Gray, Randal, ed. *Conway's All the World's Fighting Ships, 1906–1921*. London: Conway Maritime Press, 1985.

Halpern, Paul. *A Naval History of World War I*. Annapolis: Naval Institute Press, 1994.

Herwig, Holger. "The Failure of German Sea Power, 1914–1945: Mahan, Tirpitz, and Raeder Reconsidered." *International History Review* 10, no. 1 (February 1988): 68–105.

———. *The German Naval Officer Corps: A Social and Political History, 1890–1918*. Oxford: Clarendon Press, 1973.

———. *Luxury Fleet: The Imperial German Navy 1888–1918*. London: George Allen and Unwin, 1980.

Hough, Richard. *The Great War at Sea, 1914–1918*. Oxford: Oxford University Press, 1983.

Hoyt, Edwin Palmer. *Kreuzerkrieg*. Cleveland, Ohio: World Publishing, 1968.

Hubatsch, Walther. *Der Admiralstab und die obersten Marinebehörden in Deutschland*. Frankfurt: Verlag für Wehrwesen Bernhard und Graefe, 1958.

Jane, Lionel Cecil. *The Action off Heligoland, August 1914*. London: Oxford University Press, 1915.

Jarausch, Konrad H. *The Enigmatic Chancellor: Bethmann Hollweg and the Hubris of Imperial Germany*. New Haven, Conn.: Yale University Press, 1973.

Kennedy, Paul M. "The Development of German Naval Operations. Plans against England, 1896–1914." *English Historical Review* 89, no. 350 (January 1974): 48–76.

Kennedy, Paul M., ed. *The War Plans of the Great Powers, 1880–1914*. London: George Allen and Unwin, 1979.

Keynes, John, ed. *Reconstruction in Europe*. Manchester: Manchester Guardian Commercial, 1922.

King-Hall, Lady L. *Sea Saga*. London: Gollancz, 1935.

Knight, Edward F. *The Harwich Naval Forces: Their Part in the Great War*. London: Hodder and Stoughton, 1919.

Lambert, Nicholas. "British Naval Policy, 1913–1914: Financial Limitations and Strategic Revolution." *Journal of Modern History* 67 (September 1995): 595–626.

Lambi, Ivo. *The Navy and German Power Politics, 1862–1914*. Boston: Allen and Unwin, 1984.

MacDonough, Giles. *The Last Kaiser: The Life of Wilhelm II*. New York: St. Martin's Press, 2000.

Marder, Arthur. *The Anatomy of British Sea Power: A History of British Naval Policy in the Pre-Dreadnought Era, 1880–1905*. New York: Alfred Knopf, 1940.

———. *From the Dreadnought to Scapa Flow: The Royal Navy in the Fisher Era, 1904–1919*. Vol. 1: *The Road to War, 1904–1910*. London: Oxford University Press, 1961.

———. *From the Dreadnought to Scapa Flow: The Royal Navy in the Fisher Era, 1904–1919*. Vol. 2: *The War Years: To the Eve of Jutland*. London: Oxford University Press, 1965.

Massie, Robert K. *Castles of Steel: Britain, Germany, and the Winning of the Great War at Sea*. New York: Random House, 2003.

———. *Dreadnought: Britain, Germany, and the Coming of the Great War*. New York: Random House, 1991.

Murfett, Malcolm, ed. *The First Sea Lords: From Fisher to Mountbatten*. London: Praeger, 1995.

Osborne, Eric W. *Britain's Economic Blockade of Germany, 1914–1919*. London: Frank Cass, 2004.

———. *Cruisers and Battle Cruisers*. Santa Barbara, Calif.: ABC–CLIO, 2004.

Patterson, A. Temple. *Tyrwhitt of the Harwich Forces: The Life of Admiral of the Fleet Sir Reginald Tyrwhitt*. London: MacDonald, 1973.

Philbin, Tobias. *Admiral von Hipper: The Inconvenient Hero*. Amsterdam, Netherlands: B. R. Grüner, 1982.

Richmond, Herbert. *National Policy and Naval Strength*. New York: Longman's, Green, 1928.

———. *Statesmen and Seapower*. Oxford: Clarendon Press, 1946.

Ritter, Gerhard. *The Sword and the Scepter: The Problem of Militarism in Germany*. Vol. 2: *The European Powers and the Wilhelminian Empire, 1890–1914*. Trans. Heinz Norden. Coral Gables, Fla.: University of Miami Press, 1970.

———. *The Sword and the Scepter: The Problem of Militarism in Germany*. Vol. 3: *The Tragedy of Statesmanship--Bethmann Hollweg as War Chancellor (1914–1917)*. Trans. Heinz Norden. Coral Gables, Fla.: University of Miami Press, 1972.

Rodger, N. A. M. *The Admiralty*. London: Terence Dalton, 1979.

Rohl, J. C. G. "Admiral von Muller and the Approach of War, 1911–1914." *Historical Journal* 12, no. 4 (December 1969): 651–673.

Roskill, Stephen. *Admiral of the Fleet Earl Beatty: The Last Naval Hero*. New York: Atheneum, 1981.

———. *Churchill and the Admirals*. London: Collins, 1977.

Saubrei, Wolfram. *Vier goldene Sterne auf blauem Grund; Ingenohl: Eine Neuwieder Familie ein Admiral und mehr*. Neuweid: Kommissionsverlag Kehrein, 1999.

Schaefer, Theobald von. *General Staff and Admiral Staff: The Cooperation of the German Army and Navy in the World War*. Trans. Fred W. Merten. Carlisle, Pa.: Army War College, 1937.

Steinberg, Jonathan. *Yesterday's Deterrent: Tirpitz and the Birth of the German Battle Fleet*. New York: MacMillan, 1965.

———. "A German Plan for the Invasion of Holland and Belgium, 1897." *Historical Journal* 6, no. 1 (1963): 107–119.

Stokesbury, James L. *Navy and Empire*. New York: William and Morrow, 1983.

Tucker, Spencer C. *The Great War, 1914–1918*. Bloomington: Indiana University Press, 1998.

Vagts, Alfred. "Land and Sea Power in the Second German Reich." *Journal of the American Military Institute* 3, no. 4 (1939): 210–221.

Waldeyer-Hartz, Hugo von. *Admiral von Hipper*. Trans. F. Appleby Holt. London: Rich and Cowan, 1933.

Woodward, Ernest L. *Great Britain and the German Navy*. Oxford: Clarendon Press, 1935.

Woollard, Claude Lombard Aubry. *With the Harwich Naval Forces, 1914–1918; or, Under Commodore Tyrwhitt in the North Sea*. Antwerp: Kohler, 1931.

Young, Filson. *With the Battle Cruisers*. Annapolis: Naval Institute Press, 1986.

INDEX

ABOUT THE AUTHOR

ERIC W. OSBORNE is Adjunct Professor of History at Virginia Military Institute. He teaches modern European history and world history, and is author of three books that deal with diplomacy and sea power.